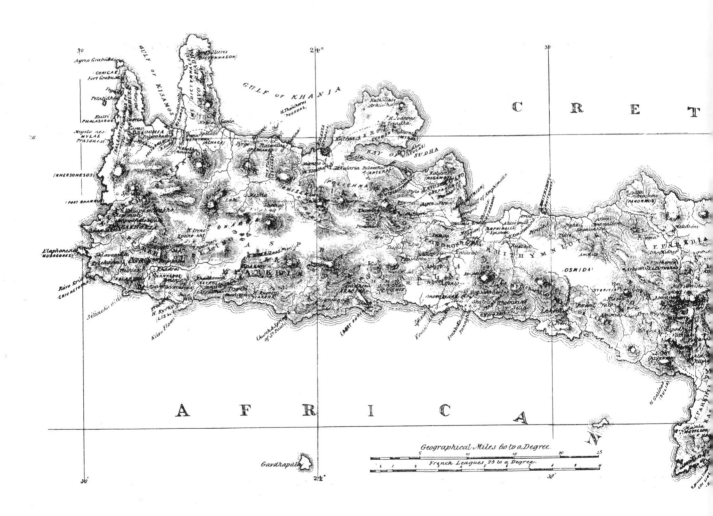

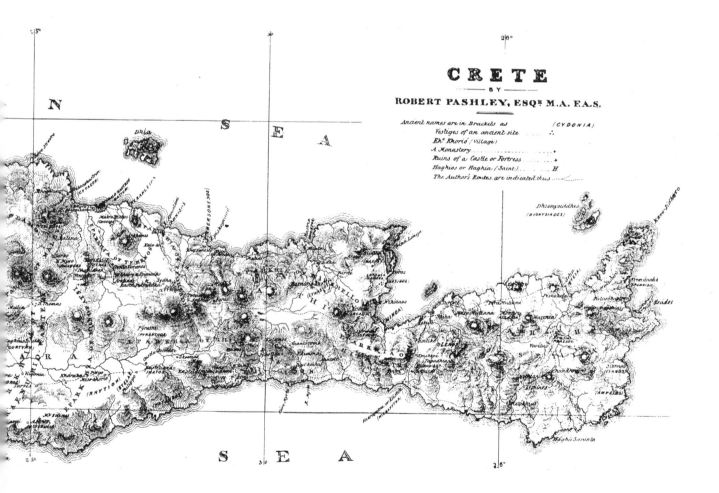

Edward Lear.

EDWARD LEAR

The Cretan Journal

EDITED BY

ROWENA FOWLER

DENISE HARVEY & COMPANY

ATHENS – DEDHAM

First published in 1984 by
Denise Harvey & Company
Lambrou Fotiadi 6, Mets, Athens, Greece
and
The Sanctuary, Dedham, Essex, England

Second edition 1985

© Denise Harvey & Company

The Cretan Journal is the seventh publication in
THE ROMIOSYNI SERIES

Phototypeset by Fotron SA
Colour separation by Katsikari Bros.
Colour printing by Dimitri Mol
Printed in Greece by K. Angelis – E. Valassakis

British Library Cataloguing in Publication Data

Lear, Edward
The Cretan journal
1. Crete – Description and travel
I. Title   II. Fowler, Rowena
914.998'043   DF901.C8

ISBN 0-907978-17-7

CONTENTS

EDITOR'S ACKNOWLEDGEMENTS

I would like to thank Vivien Noakes for so generously sharing with me her expert knowledge of all aspects of Edward Lear's life and work. For their help with the preparation of this edition I would also like to thank: Eleanor Garvey (Houghton Library, Harvard); Ruth Pitman, Pat Rogers (University of Bristol); Philip Sherrard; Bernard Silverman; Fani-Maria Tsigakou (Benaki Museum, Athens); Francis Walton and Sophia Papageorgiou (Gennadius Library, Athens); Elizabeth Warren; and my publisher, Denise Harvey. For permission to reproduce drawings or to quote from unpublished material I am grateful to: The Gennadius Library (pp. 27, 55, 59, 60, 61, 62, 63, 66, 67, 69, 75, 76, 78, 83, 84, 85, 95 (top), 97, 98, 99, 101, 103, 104); Mrs Maro Seferiades (pp. 25, 48); Mr Patrick Leigh Fermor (pp. 39, 47, 53, 57, 95 (bottom), 96); The Trustees of the British Museum (p. 100); The National Art Gallery of New Zealand (p. 42); The Ashmolean Museum (pp. 31, 87, 91); The Toledo Museum of Art (p. 29); The Museum of Art, Rhode Island School of Design (p. 35); Thomas Agnew & Sons Ltd. (p. 50); The Radio Times Hulton Picture Library (frontispiece); Mr Humphrey Nevill (p. 33); Miss Prescott and the late Col. W. Prescott (pp. 44, 72, 93); The Houghton Library (pp. 21, 22); The National Portrait Gallery, London (p. 68); The County Archivist, Somerset Record Office (letters of Lear to Chichester Fortescue and Lady Waldegrave); Lord Tennyson and the Lincolnshire Library Service (letter to Emily Tennyson); the Rt Hon. The Lord Aberdare and the Glamorgan Record Office (letter to Henry Bruce). The photographs of the drawings in the Gennadius Library and in the private collections of Mrs Seferiades and Mr Leigh Fermor were taken by Eugene Vanderpool; and the map of Crete (pp. 118–9) is reproduced by kind permission of the artist, Roger Bedding.

INTRODUCTION

When Edward Lear set out for Crete from Corfu in April 1864, it was in no very optimistic frame of mind. Off and on for the last nine years he had made his winter home in Corfu and, in spite of sometimes being lonely and depressed, he had grown fond of the island. Now, after half a century of British rule, Corfu and the other Ionian islands had been ceded to Greece, and the British community was dispersing. As Lear watched the garrison leaving and the fortifications being demolished, he forgot his past irritations — the noisy neighbours, the pettinesses of colonial society — and began to feel nostalgic for what he knew he would miss: the lovely walks and views, the people whose company he enjoyed.

Lear was then fifty-one. He had been born into a comfortably-off London family in 1812, the twentieth of twenty-one children. The family fell on hard times, and Lear, never a happy child, began at an early age to suffer from the epileptic attacks, bronchial troubles and tendency to depression which were to trouble him for the rest of his life. From the age of fifteen to his death in 1888 he earned his living as an artist. Between 1832 and 1836 he was employed by Lord Edward Stanley, heir to the twelfth Earl of Derby, to draw the animals and birds in the menagerie at Knowsley Hall near Liverpool. In his spare time, to amuse the children of the family, he began making the Nonsense drawings and verses for which he is so well known today. After leaving Knowsley Lear concentrated on landscape painting, and travelled widely in Europe and the Near East, and as far afield as Ceylon and India, in search of new and unusual scenes. He never married. The external details of his life are well documented from his letters and diaries. Vivien Noakes's standard biography offers a fascinating account of Lear's life and career, and of the society in which he moved and from which he periodically escaped.

Lear's inability to settle in one place was partly obsessional, the result of dissatisfaction with his life and work, but the move from Corfu was forced on him by outside circumstances. It was a problem to decide where to go next. His health required a permanent winter home where he could escape the fogs and damp of London; his livelihood, on the other hand, required an immediate expedition to somewhere exotic where he could discover new scenes. Crete was one possibility for such an expedition, and was first mooted in a letter to Lear's friend Chichester Fortescue on 7 February 1864: 'Whether I go to Albania — or Syria — or to [illegible] or Crete — or Asia Minor — is dark. Fools ask — why to any? — supposing that the same subjects as paintings can be sold over and over again.' An expedition to Crete had the advantage that it could also be combined with an exploratory visit to Athens, which was one of the places Lear was considering as a possible home for the future. The decision was soon made. By the middle of March he had marked in his diary his expected date of arrival in Athens, and was reading Robert Pashley's *Travels in Crete*, which was to be his constant companion for the next two months.

Crete was in some ways a natural choice. Subscriptions for Lear's last book, *Views in the Seven Ionian Islands,* had come in slowly but steadily, and he probably felt that another book of Mediterranean travels would be likely to sell. He had also cherished, since his first visit to Greece in 1848, the idea of one day collecting his journals and sketches into a general 'Topography of Greece', and the idea was revived in a letter to Fortescue on 31 March 1864: 'Crete it seems is on the list of destinies, & being part of my polygraphic Hellenic proclivities is one of the things necessary to be done.' Furthermore, the island had various intrinsic attractions. It was still remote enough to be an unhackneyed subject for an artist and travel writer and it contained mediaeval and Venetian buildings as well as some ancient sites. The Minoan palaces which have since made Crete a major tourist centre were not unearthed until the early twentieth century. In 1864 the most famous Cretan antiquities were Aptera (mainly Hellenistic) and Gortyn (Roman), both of which Lear visited and drew, and it seems odd nowadays to read that he found only a few 'scattered masses of brickwork' at Knossos (p. 66) and that he walked straight over the sites of Phaestos and Aghia Triádha.

One other possible reason for choosing Crete was that Lear enjoyed his travels better when he could communicate with the people he met. He had begun to study modern Greek in 1848 and could read and speak it reasonably well. While living in Corfu he had regular lessons although his occasional phonetic misspellings suggest that he also took in a good deal by ear. He liked playing with the language, making up Greek poems and nonsense words; he even attempted a serious translation into Greek of Tennyson's poem 'Will'. He scattered Greek words and phrases throughout his diaries and letters and sometimes composed whole letters in Greek. He wrote in the modern semi-cursive script, which has proved a problem for some of his readers. (The editor of the *Letters,* baffled by Lear's Greek, referred it to classical scholars who pronounced it 'atrocious'. In the Preface to the second edition of the book, however, an apologetic note explained that it was in fact *modern* Greek, and offered corrections for the more conspicuously mistaken translations.) Lear enjoyed Greek for its own sake but he also appreciated the practical value of languages: 'It will be good fun when I can understand Greek well', he wrote to his sister in 1856, 'as I can then get many things more as the natives do, than after the extravagant English modes.'

Lear was a seasoned traveller; his advice on packing had proved practical enough to be incorporated in early editions of John Murray's famous *Handbook for Travellers in Greece.* Before setting off for Crete he got out his camp-bed, hat-box and saddlebags and assembled what he had learned from experience was the bare minimum:

> . . . a certain supply of cooking utensils, tin plates, knives and forks, a basin, &c . . . . A light mattress, some sheets and blankets, and a good supply of capotes and plaids should not be neglected; two or three books; some rice, curry-powder, and cayenne; a world of drawing materials . . . ; as little dress as possible, though you must have two sets of outer clothing — one for visiting consuls, pashás, and dignitaries, the other for rough,

everyday work; some quinine made into pills (rather leave all behind than this) . . .

Journals of a Landscape Painter in Albania, p. 7

He obtained letters of introduction to consuls, officials and community leaders who might be able to help him and put him up, for only in an emergency would he fall back on a public inn or *khan* ('so called because one tries to live there but *can't*').

Lear left Corfu for Athens on 4 April, travelling via Syra (Syros), which before the cutting of the Corinth Canal was an important centre for all Aegean shipping. It was sixteen years since he had last been that way and he looked forward to seeing Athens again. The city had grown almost out of recognition but some of Lear's old acquaintances were still there, in the somewhat claustrophobic expatriate community. He realised almost at once that Athens would not do to settle in and he concentrated on getting things ready for Crete, where he arrived, in a rainstorm, on 11 April.

In 1864 Crete was still part of European Turkey. Of a population of some 200,000, roughly three-quarters (mainly Greeks) were Orthodox Christians and a quarter (mainly Turks, with some Albanians, Arabs and Negroes) were Moslems. It was, however, no easy matter to distinguish between 'Greeks' and 'Turks': intermarriage was quite common, a number of Greeks had converted to Islam, most Turks in the countryside spoke only Greek, and even the urban Turks thought of themselves as Cretans first and foremost. Albanian was, after Greek, the most widely spoken language; Albanians policed the island and were important in local administration. The Arab immigrants living in villages of tents outside Rethymnon and Haniá had come from the Benghazi area in the 1830s when Crete was ruled for a while from Egypt, and the 'blacks' Lear was to comment on had been brought by the Egyptians as slaves and soldiers, and had stayed on in their flat-roofed village under the walls of Haniá. Both these communities spoke Arabic. There were also Jews, Armenians and Maltese who, with Greeks from nearby Cythera (Cerigo), handled much of the island's trade.

As in his earlier Balkan travels, Lear comments impartially on costumes, customs, individuals. He had not received a classical education and although he had been an admirer of Byron and although he worked hard at his modern Greek, his outlook was free from the prejudices of Romantic philhellenism. His letters show that he was much concerned about the 'Eastern Question' and attempted to discuss it without falling into the blind partisanship which bedevilled certain British politicians: 'Now, no one has ever heard me say a word in favour of the Turks as Government or Governors. I always "held them abominable". But there is a wide difference between that opinion, and the stirring up bad and narrow feeling by screaming that "all Turks are unmentionable and brutes" . . . On the contrary, the mass of the Turkish people — not their governors — is honest and noble . . .' (*Later Letters*, p. 229).

Lear was aware of the political tensions in Crete. He was struck by the ruined and neglected appearance of the countryside which was partly the result of earthquakes, depopulation and bad government but also due to uprisings — in the years 1821–7, 1841 and 1858 — of the Greeks against their Turkish overlords. Only two years after Lear's visit to the monastery of Arkádhi it was to go up in smoke, and with it his host, the abbot Gabriel Marinákis, during the most renowned and violent of the island's uprisings. Besieged by the forces of Mustafa Pasha, the Cretan insurgents in the monastery put a light to their powder magazine, choosing to kill themselves and the enemy rather than surrender. It is said that Gabriel himself gave the fateful order. Lear had seen war and revolution before: in Sicily in 1847 and on the Italian mainland in 1848 and 1859. In spite of his lively interest in events he aimed when travelling to 'studiously avoid politics' — a difficult task in Greece.

Although Crete was off the beaten track for pilgrims and Grand Tourists, it had attracted British merchants, explorers and antiquarians since the sixteenth century, and some of the early travellers have left valuable and amusing accounts of the island. In some ways Lear is closer to them than he is to the self-consciously elegant travellers of the eighteenth century or to the standard authorities of his own time, Pashley and Spratt. Robert Pashley's two-volume *Travels in Crete* (1837) was the most comprehensive account available to Lear. Although it was never intended as a practical guide and its descriptions of the contemporary landscape were already rather out of date, it was a useful book to have in one's saddlebag. Pashley identified and described many of the ancient sites that were then visible. He was concerned with the general conditions of life on the island and was particularly interested in the survival of ancient practices and traditions into the nineteenth century. He was also a valuable ice-breaker: Lear met people in Crete who still remembered the English scholar's visit thirty years before, and when conversation with his Greek hosts flagged he could always fall back on reading out relevant passages from the *Travels* in extempore translation. Captain T. A. B. Spratt had surveyed the coast of Crete for the British Admiralty in the early 1850s and his findings were published in the *Mediterranean Pilot*. He had also travelled in the interior of the island, but although his resultant map of Crete was available to Lear (see p. 31) his written account was not published until 1865, the year after Lear's trip. Spratt, like Pashley, was interested in the identification of classical sites, but his main concerns were cartography and meteorology. He met some of the same people Lear was to meet later, but insisted on travelling with his own tent to avoid staying overnight in Cretan houses. He quotes appreciatively from earlier travellers, and especially from William Lithgow's *Rare Adventures and Painefull Peregrinations* of 1632. Lear got hold of Spratt's book as soon as it came out but missed the benefit of having it with him on the spot.

Lear, in his Cretan journal, is less comprehensive and more personal than either Pashley or Spratt. He offers us, first, a detailed and sometimes minute-by-minute commentary on the landscape of Crete and, second, an impression of the ups and downs, physical and mental, of an artist travelling on foot over difficult country. He is good on people, food, birds and flowers, disappointing on language, literature and local culture; he notes a few dialect words but, although he knew Fauriel's *Chants*

12

populaires de la Grèce moderne (1824–5) he makes no mention of any folk music or poetry. The weather was generally foul, and in the evening the rigours of Cretan hospitality matched the physical strain of the day's travelling.

Although Lear was sometimes cantankerous he was also remarkably resilient: a good meal, fine weather, an unexpectedly clear view or pleasant encounter never failed to put him in good spirits. He was lucky in his servant Giorgio, or George Kokáli (the Suliot, as Lear often called him), who had already been with Lear for eight years and was to spend the rest of his life in his employment. George was a resourceful valet and cook and an equable travelling companion. Best of all, he could share his master's verbal jokes and sometimes amused Lear with his own rather stoical brand of humour.

Another bonus was the dignity and courtesy of the Cretans. Lear's surprise at the least manifestation of ordinary politeness was the legacy of his travels in Albania where he had been treated as a devil, freak or spy. His sketching did elicit some measure of suspicion from the Turkish authorities in Crete but the islanders themselves turned out to be tolerant, respectful and even admiring. The Cretan dogs also made a good impression on Lear, who frequently contrasts them with the 'legions of odious hounds' that were always snapping at his heels in Albania. Altogether, he enjoyed a general sense of security — from theft, interference or assault. He also comments on other features which visitors to rural Crete today will immediately recognise: the vagueness about distances, the perpetual questions, the sudden gifts, the fierce local patriotism.

Lear's primary interest, however, was in landscape, and landscape seen from his particular point of view. His ideas of what constituted a paintable scene were based on earlier eighteenth- and nineteenth-century traditions of landscape painting, but he most frequently cites in his Cretan journal the old masters Claude Lorraine and Raphael. Crete was difficult to accommodate to preconceived ideas of beauty; it was too vast, too rugged and raw, and Lear was constantly frustrated by the lack of 'drawable', well-composed scenes. He compares Crete unfavourably with Corfu and Sicily — sometimes unfairly, in that his aesthetic judgements are influenced by memories of times when he was younger and happier.

The classic account of Lear's method of sketching is given by his friend and protégé Hubert Congreve in his Preface to the *Later Letters:*

> When we came to a good subject, Lear would sit down, and taking his block from George, would lift his spectacles, and gaze for several minutes at the scene through a monocular glass he always carried; then, laying down the glass, and adjusting his spectacles, he would put on paper the view before us, mountain range, villages and foreground, with a rapidity and accuracy that inspired me with awestruck admiration.

Lear then scribbled notes on these preliminary sketches and numbered them; later, indoors, he would 'pen out', inking over his pencil outlines.

At the same time he was keeping a journal, writing in pen in his Letts diary whenever he stopped to draw or rest or to have lunch. Sometimes the day's entry would be finished in bed at night, if he had enough light and not too many disturbances. His travels in Albania and in Southern Italy had been written up from the detailed letters he sent to his sister Ann, but Ann's death in 1861 meant that he no longer wrote a full account for any one correspondent. Thus, on the Cretan expedition, it was his diary that became the basis for the book he hoped later to publish.

What did Lear intend such a book to be? In the Preface to *Journals of a Landscape Painter in Corsica* he suggests that the words are ancillary to the illustrations themselves — 'to be aids to the knowledge of scenery which I have visited and delineated' — but this does not mean that the written accounts are sketchy: to his friend Fortescue he described the first of his Egyptian journals as 'photographically minute and truthful'. In the account of Crete, words and pictures often go together beautifully: the diary entry on 24 May, for instance, suggests that Lear knew his views of Mount Ida from Phré were the best work he achieved in Crete. The diary often gives a verbal impression of a particular scene, while the notes written on the drawings themselves, which include some delightfully nonsensical phonetic spellings, fill out the written account. Many diary entries refer to specific sketches, adding details of form and colour, cross references to other scenes or a re-assessment of a scene already drawn. Conversely, the drawings were to be an important aide-mémoire for Lear's finished book: 'see drawing', he writes, or 'reflect from your sketches'. But sometimes it is hard to believe the same man did both — at Haniá on 19 April the diary is mainly a list of grumbles, while the drawing of the water-front is one of his best.

Today's readers, more familiar with the Lear of the Nonsense books, tend to be primarily interested in the travel journals for what they may tell us about his personality as man and writer. What has the diary of the 'topographical artist' in common with his other writings? There are the idiosyncratic spellings and rather weak puns that we know from the letters and the Nonsense. There is the strong sense of the incongruous — of the juxtaposition of a jug of rosebuds with a box of 'macaroni-like' silkworms — and, beyond that, the hint of social unease and existential despair. Lear's mind was all of a piece; there is more homogeneity in his writing than we find, for instance, in the work of 'Lewis Carroll' and the *Journal of a Tour in Russia in 1867* of Charles Lutwidge Dodgson. We see it in the Cretan diary in the encounters with grotesque human beings and recalcitrant animals, in the situations where people drink out of a candlestick, take flea powder for snuff or kill lice with the coffee pot. Lear, like the characters in his Nonsense verses, is often bored, stared at or plied with disgusting food. Indeed, the verses seem almost prophetic: Nonsense characters had been eating snails since the 1840s. And on the sketch of Rethymnon made on 26 May Lear quotes the lines he had published three years before in the new edition of *A Book of Nonsense*: 'There was a young person of Crete / Whose toilette was far from complete . . .'.

The diary, more so even than the letters, gives us an occasional direct glimpse into Lear's thoughts and emotions, which are most often wistful and full of nostalgia. Fatigue and physical discomfort at least spurred him into lively expressions of irritation and it is when he is temporarily relaxed and in beautiful surroundings that he is overtaken by his Tennysonian sense of 'Tears, idle tears'. But there are no startling revelations, and the Cretan diary confirms rather than alters the impression of Lear's personality that we get from his already published work and from the researches of his biographers.

True to form, Lear began to get attached to Crete when it was time to leave, and he knew he would miss the easy hospitality of Consul Hay and his family, his hosts at Halépa. A letter to Emily Tennyson written on 31 July after his return mentions Mrs Hay — 'the most beautifullest and fascinatingest of Spanish ladies' — and the Tennyson songs they used to sing together in the evenings. In his diary he remembers 'those happy bright Crete & Corfu days' and records that his servant George is urging another visit to their favourite picnic place at Zitso, outside Rethymnon: 'Let us go again to Crete — Zitso, Zitso.'

Although he refers in his Corsican journal, which was published six years after his Cretan expedition, to 'that far-off indefinite time when I may wind up my journeys in Crete, Palestine, Syria, and other only-in-part-visited places', it is unlikely that Lear ever seriously intended to return. Of the places he had planned to 'do', only Sphakiá had eluded him; he had seen the three main towns and all the major sights of Western Crete and had brought away with him almost two hundred sketches.

After arriving back in England, on 11 June, Lear had to get down to sorting out and making what he could of his material, a task he detested. While still in Crete he had begun writing up a fair copy of his diary — we know he had re-written at least as far as 15 May by the time he left Haniá — and he continued to work on it in England during the summer. Throughout June and July he was penning out and colouring the Cretan sketches, '196 drawings — & a vast number of small bits', until on 24 August he could write in his diary, 'The Cretan labour is done'. Then, at the beginning of November, he set off for the South of France. New concerns crowded in on him and we hear little of the progress of the Crete book, though he still intended to publish it one day: 'I could wish to publish 2 little volumes — Crete & The Corniche as to my 1864 doings', he wrote to Fortescue on 24 February 1865.

It was probably reading about the 1866 uprising in Crete that brought the island back into the forefront of Lear's mind. His first diary note of it is on 19 September: 'There has been bloodshed in Crete — ahi ἡμέρας περασμένας! [byegone days].' Odd bits of news filtered through to him on his travels that winter and he talked about the progress of the uprising with consuls and beys he met in Egypt. On 29 April 1867 he found himself on a boat off the coast of Crete on the way home from a journey up the Nile:

Noon — atmosphere thicker but Crete plainly visible. — the outline &

snow of Ida & the Sphakia range becoming by degrees forcible. 3 to 4 — I gaze on the Island ever — seeing the low grounds of Ida — where we passed over to Ἀποδοῦλο [Apodhoúlo] — what miseries now are in that sad island! There are the White Mountains — there are all the familiar forms! . . . When at 5.30 I came up to the fore-deck — we were just passing 'Gozo di Candia' [Gavdhos] a bare rock. Afterwards sitting with G. [George] — we talked over the Crete days of 1864 — watching the great line of the Sphakian hills & the Selinos district, & the long points of land running out northerly — till it was 7 o'clock, & we steam away from the Island: — tho', even were we nearer to it, darkness would prevent us seeing it. Yet I think I see the farthest N.W. promontery near Kissamos, & perhaps a part of that nearer Goniá. It is curious to remember the rough yet pleasant life I led here 3 years ago! —

Back in England, Lear wrote out his Nile journal while it was fresh in his mind, but the minute it was finished he turned back to Crete, beginning the project at Lord Northbrook's house in Hampshire on 28 August 1867: '. . . about to try a little journalizing of Crete — sad as it is to me to do so.' He went on with the journal regularly that autumn taking it with him to the Drummonds at Cadland, the Tennysons at Farringford, to Sir John Simeon at Swainston and finally into lodgings at Cannes, where the weather was cold but dazzlingly sunny and he had to write with the blinds closed. The work was slow and hard on the eyes and it was a poignant task to copy out descriptions of places and people knowing they had been overtaken by events: 'poor Crete!' he wrote in his diary on 30 November; and on 17 December, 'I wish I could know if poor Κοσταντί [Konstandís] is alive'. The worst thing was regretting sights he had skimped or not appreciated at the time and which had now gone for good: 'The Crete journal writing saddens me horribly — especially of the Ἀρκάδι [Arkádhi] visit . . .'.

The journal was finished at last on Christmas Eve 1867 and he immediately embarked on preparing another — of an earlier visit to Egypt in 1854. Both diary and letters show that Lear had a strong sense of the importance of a lifetime's work which could be seen as a whole: that is why he kept his papers so carefully and why he was always planning ambitious (though never-to-be-completed) projects such as sets of illustrations to Tennyson's poems, or a complete photographic record of all his own pictures. The travel books were a part of this overall conception: 'At present', he wrote to Lady Waldegrave on 9 January 1868,

I am not drawing at all nor painting — but writing: the rough copy of my Cretan journals is done — & nearly that of the Nile 1854 — : the Nubia of 1867 will follow — & I mean to get all 3 ready for publication with illustrations — if possible next summer — whether in parts — or volumes I can't yet say. By degrees I want to topographize & typographize all the journeyings of my life — so that I shall have been of some use after all to my fellow critters — besides leaving them drawings & pictures which they may sell when I'm dead.

Yet instead of getting the three journals ready for publication he spent the early summer of 1868 in Corsica, and the rest of the year writing up his travels there. He was plagued with frustrations at every stage of the publication of *Journal of a Landscape Painter in Corsica* — the preparation of the illustrations was particularly difficult — and when the book did come out, in 1870, it was not a great success. Even so, Lear never gave up his resolve, writing to Fortescue, for instance, on 31 July 1870:

> I should certainly like, as I grow old, (if I do at all, —) to work out & complete my topographic life — publishing all my journals illustrated, & illustrations of all my pictures: for after all if a man does *anything* *all* his life & is not a dawdler, — what he does *must* be worth something — even if only as a lesson of perseverance.

But no more of Lear's travels were to appear in print in his lifetime, even — a possibility he had always kept in reserve — as extracts in magazines.

At his death in 1888 several of the unpublished journals were among the carefully preserved papers left for his friend and executor Franklin Lushington. Many of these papers were subsequently destroyed, lost or dispersed. The original diary for 1864 is extant but all that remains of Lear's various later versions of the Cretan journal is a manuscript of fifty-six pages (4 April – 4 May), all lightly scored through as if a new copy had been made. This is probably the old fair copy he had made in 1864 and which he heavily emended in 1867 as a preliminary to complete re-writing. In several places Lear makes the common error of substituting the current year for the date of writing: 1867 for 1864. What became of the other fifty or so pages and what happened to the new fair copy, if there was one, is not known.

Comparison of this journal fragment with the original diary gives us an idea of how Lear intended to prepare his material for publication. Jottings are expanded, grammar and syntax tidied up, unpleasant details toned down and personal remarks removed. Grumbles tend to give way to a bluff heartiness. The later version is more polite, more discursive and less spontaneous. The hasty impressionism of the diary (which at its best, as on page 16, has a rhythm of its own) is smoothed out into the somewhat ponderous style one finds in the published travel books. That Lear knew he was over-writing is clear from a margin note on the later version of the fight on board the *Persia*: 'the other account is best'. The odd words in Greek that are a habit throughout the diary, a kind of verbal doodling, are removed in the later version and personal names tend to be replaced by initials. Margin notes in the fragment ('generalize', 'condense', 'quote', 'check', 'amalgamate') as well as question-marks and bracketed alternatives show that another copy was at least planned. There were still points to be cleared up: against the journal entry for 3 May, for example, there is a note to 'ask Adml R. [Admiral Sir Robert Spencer Robinson] about Suda Bay'.

The finished book would have had a map — 'see map', he writes — but it is hard to know what sort of illustrations Lear had in mind. Four 'wood cuts' are indicated in the margin at the beginning of the journal; would these have been for vignettes of the picturesque Albanian Gheges and the Montenegrins he saw on the boat, or was he thinking of reproducing his landscapes by the process of wood engraving he had experimented with in the Corsica journal? He had used various types of lithographic reproduction in the earlier travel books and this was the method he was most at home with. Collectors have increasingly come to prefer the spontaneity of the original sketches, as reproduced here, although they were never intended for sale or publication. Their light colours and lines are fresher and more attractive than the 'lithotints' of the Albania volume or the literal, over-worked paintings he later turned out to order. Lear bequeathed the sketches to Franklin Lushington, and they came on to the London market in 1929, after Lushington's death. Ninety-two of the Cretan sketches are now in the Gennadius Library in Athens, a few are in other libraries and museums and the rest are in private collections.

Lear based a few finished watercolours on the sketches he made in Crete but, so far as one can tell, no oils or lithographs. Although he started to 'work up' two of these watercolours before he left Haniá (see p. 102) his interest seems to have flagged later as Crete proved difficult to sell. (He gave away 'Haniá Gate' as a wedding present.) The problem was that Lear's clients tended to commission paintings of scenes or places they had themselves visited, or hoped to visit or had at least heard of; Crete failed to appeal as much as Italy, mainland Greece or even Egypt or India. In the end it was only his San Remo neighbour, the Revd Henry Tozer, who chose Crete. Tozer seems to have been pleased with his picture of Ghoniá, commissioned in 1872. He went to Crete himself two years later and on his return bought paintings of Haniá, Ida and Arkádhi. All four watercolours were subsequently bequeathed to the Ashmolean Museum. Lear also made a pen and ink drawing of Plataniá, to illustrate Tennyson's line 'Flowing like a crystal river'.

Lear included a preface in most of his travel books in which he described his aims and methods. In his Cretan journal he would certainly have referred to Pashley and to Spratt and might have incorporated extracts from such standard authors to pad out his own account, as he did in the 'Additional Notes' to his Corsica book. He added a postscript to *Southern Calabria and the Kingdom of Naples,* describing from magazine accounts the earthquake of 1851 which had destroyed many of the places he had visited there in 1848. Might he have added a postscript about the 1866 uprising in Crete? There is no way of knowing whether or not he had such a thing in mind, if indeed he got as far as thinking about such details. But he would have been amused to think of a later generation collating and hypothesising over his rough drafts and relieved, I hope, that someone else had taken on the task of preparing them for publication.

Rowena Fowler

TEXTUAL NOTE

The text is that of Lear's diary, now in the Houghton Library at Harvard (Ms Eng 797.3 (v.7)).

I have expanded abbreviations and regularized spelling while retaining Lear's intentional misspellings. Lear's original punctuation has also been retained except in the case of dashes, many of which have been removed or replaced with other appropriate punctuation marks. Multiple exclamation marks are generally reduced to one. Table and room plans have been omitted.

Incidental words and names in Greek have in the main been replaced by English translations or transliterations, while dialogue and local terms have been retained, with spellings, accents and breathings regularized. Greek place names are always a problem: Lear's practice is not consistent and he sometimes even mixes English and Greek letters in the same word. My own solution has been to use accepted English forms where these exist, otherwise to use forms demoticized and transliterated from the *Megáli Ellinikí Enkyklopaidheía,* with the stress marked unless it falls on the first syllable.

Additions to the text are of two kinds: 1. Words, names, dates and translations which I have supplied — these are enclosed in square brackets. 2. Substantive variations or additional explanatory material from Lear's incomplete 'fair copy' of the Cretan journal (Houghton Library bMS Typ 55.14) — these are enclosed in double square brackets.

Dates in the text are those of Lear's English (Letts) diary and therefore twelve days later than dates in Greece and Turkey, where the Julian calendar was still in use. This explains why, for instance, Lear saw a firework display in Athens on 6 April — it was the Greek 25 March, the feast day of the Annunciation and official anniversary of the Greek War of Independence.

Times are important in the text. From Lear's careful recording of the state of the light it can be calculated that his watch was within a few minutes of solar time and therefore varying about $1^{1}/_{2}$ hours from present-day Greek Summer Time.

R. F.

The Journal

LETTS'S Nº 8 DIARY

1864

Weather fine – but strongish N. Wind. Everything was ready as early
as I could manage, & G. took the last things away to Spiro's room.
So only 11 packages for the voyage remained. Wandered about
miserably – & had to get one or 2 little things at
Cuzzaris' & Taylor's. Walking up the streets – spoke to Politi; who thinks all the
Jews will go sooner or later. At 12.40 to Dr Vees – returned with them
for the last time. Came away at 2 – & came yet 3 with George
& Spiro in a boat to the ——— Lloyd's "Stadieon". (Saw Capt.
Daniele – & heard that all the 10 little pens were dead or stolen.)
I'ed enough on do but in better spirits than when I went last year,
for evelyn Baring joined me soon after, had S. or left Corfu. –
Once more I left the loveliest place in the world – with a pang –
tho' less this time this not being alone.   Dinner – wafts, Ba &
walked talked smoked & sat till 8 – when there was tea – & then –
& the sloppying the G. – when we went to bed. Slept till 10.30 – but the
rolling & cracking of the ship when up——— ————— ——— filled me beyond
———— bored & worried me terribly!   Later it grew calmer, &
I slept from 12.45 – to 6.15 – when G. woke me.

She sits upon her Bulbul
    Through the long long hours of night –
And ——— the dark hinges gleams
    ——— o'er The Yashmak's fitful light.
The lonely Gardener sails slowly down
    The steep or craggy dell –
And from his lofty nest, loud screams
    The white plumed Asphodel.

|| alas! indeed Yes! –

(12 Aug 1865)
    Yesterday H de Vere
        was killed.

Weather fine, but strongish north wind. Everything was ready as early as I could manage, and George took the last things away to Spiro's[1] room. So only the eleven packages for the voyage remained. Wandered about miserably, and had to get one or two little things at Courage's and Taylor's. Walking up the Ghetto, spoke to Políti, who thinks all the Jews will go sooner or later.[2] At 12.40 to De Vere's, and lunched with them for the *last* time.[3] Came away at two, and came off at three with George and Spiro in a boat to the Austrian Lloyd's *Stadium*. (Saw Captain Deverill, and heard that all the ten little geese were dead or stolen.)[4] Sad enough am I, but in better spirits than when I went last year, for Evelyn Baring[5] joined me soon after and at five we left Corfu. Once more I left the loveliest place in the world, with a pang, though less this time through not being alone. Dinner, and afterwards Baring and I walked, talked, smoked and sat till eight, when there was tea, and then we sat star-gazing till nine, when we went to bed. Slept till 10.30, but the rolling and cracking of the ship when we got out into full sea beyond Paxos bored and worried me terribly: later it grew calmer, and I slept from 12.45 to 6.15, when George woke me.

> She sits upon her Bulbul
>   Through the long long hours of night,
> And o'er the dark horizon gleams
>   The Yashmack's fitful light.
> The lone Yaourt sails slowly down
>   The deep and craggy dell,
> And from his lofty nest, loud screams
>   The white plumed Asphodel.[6]

Very lovely morning. Dressed and on deck by seven. Mount Skopó is fast fading, so we must have made Zante about in twelve hours, and therefore may be off Cerigo [Cythera] by 5 or 6 p.m. The lines of Morea hills are very lovely. Walked till nine, and sat with Baring, till 10. Breakfast. Navarino, Sapienza, Modon, Coron, Cabrera, views of Taygetus, etc. Venetico at twelve: sea and sky lovely. All day on deck; more movement near Matapan. Taygetus very grand, and Cerigo in sight before dinner. Afterwards, Cape St Angelo very grand, and all Cerigo spread abroad: the classic lines of Cythera, and the village of Potamó. The hermit of St Angelo. Walked up and down till eleven. Rougher night, but slept at times.

At Syra by five. The old sparkly pile once more. On board the *Oriente* by 7.30, with all our traps, leaving the gay Gheges and flannel-clothed Montenegrins and the small lemon-coloured child, for a vessel not so large as the *Stadium,* and with few passengers.

SYRA
AT SEA
PIRAEUS
ATHENS

We did not start till nine, after endless dawdle-merchant delays. A brisk north breeze, but I enjoyed being pretty well, and seeing those 'Isles of Greece' again, bare as they are: Delos, Tinos and Andros, and by twelve (after breakfast and talk with Baring) Cythnos; and later the long Ceos (whereabouts, getting into open sea, the waves were rough and rolling), and Euboea dim about four. Then Makrónisos, and towards sunset the most beautiful Colonna [Sounion], unseen by me since 1849. It grew stormy towards 6.30, and dark, but we got into Piraeus harbour by 7.30 or 7.45. Here were rockets and patriotism, but no bother for us, for we were closely put in a boat, and two coaches and by 9.15 — lo! — Baring and I, and afterwards the Suliot and luggage, were at Athens! Rest and be thankful. Cleaning [[in comfortable rooms at the Hotel]] [de la Couronne] and (Baring having gone to Mr Scarlett's[7] and at ten returned) we had some supper and went to bed at eleven.

THURSDAY
7 APRIL

ATHENS

Rose at 5.30. Day fine. How strange to see the Acropolis once more! and the long lines of Piraeus! Rose, and made out washing lists and arranged luggage. At 8.30 walked out with George, and a guide — for I had forgotten the houses and streets. Very odd are the recollections of 1848–9! To Mr Hill's,[8] sending in my photograph. Mr Hill is as usual; hardly altered, though according to him 75. Mrs Hill seems more aged. Knowing of my letter to an A.D.C. of the King, he *would* make me go and deliver it to Count Sponnek.[9] To General Church[10] — Finlay[11] — but neither up; so I walked with George to the Jupiter Olympus (one column down since 1849) and then partly up Lycabettus, whence one saw how greatly the town is increased. Returning, called on Finlay, on General Sir Richard Church and again on the Hills, this time seeing Mrs Hill, and to Mr Scarlett. Returned at 12.30 and breakfasted with Evelyn Baring, after which (having avoided Campbell Johnston,[12] whom also I saw in the Palace) Baring and I dawdled away time till 2.30, when we drove to Colonus and the Theseum, and so by the Areopagus to the Acropolis. 5.30 p.m. walking there and seeing the WONDERFUL! newly excavated theatre of Bacchus, and so by Jupiter Olympus, back by the Eolus Street by 6.30–45. Dined, not unpleasantly. Evelyn Baring is now — 10 p.m. — gone out to the theatre. George comes, having bought padlocks, and being generally cheerful: and now — at 10.15 — I am going to bed. Awfully cold.

FRIDAY
8 APRIL

ATHENS

Horridly cold, and so cloudy that we gave up all idea of going up Lycabettus. Packed for Crete, 7–9.30. Breakfast. Letter from T. Cooper,[13] enclosing one from Drummond:[14] payments of £12.12s (Mrs Mildmay)

£21.00s (Capt. Lawson)

£33.12s

As Baring and I were going out — lo! — *potius aper* Campbell Johnston, of whom we could only get rid by Mr Hill's door. We sat a while with Mr Hill, and got home — half frozen — by 12.30. Wrote to Ellen,[15] Mrs George Clive,[16] Lawson and T. Cooper. General Church called, which I was vexed at — at 82! — that he should come up three pairs of stairs: Baring went to the Βουλή [Parliament] and I read the *Observer*:

24

Athens, painted by Lear on his previous visit in 1848–9.

Mrs D. Nevill[17] is dead, (71). At three Baring and I walked to the Theseum, and Museum, and Philopappus, and Ilissus and 'Lantern',[18] and home; the cold being *frightful*: dark, gloomy sky and cutting east wind. Then, about five, we went to Constantin's[19] and saw photographs (beautiful) and returned by six to dress.

At seven to the Legation. The 'Staff' are a bore: discontented, vain, ridiculous; abusing this place and these people, as such fools do all places, and all peoples. The Scarlett family seemed really a delightful lot — natural and kindly. The effort made by Mr Scarlett to keep the 'Staff' from killing a poor centipede would alone have made me like him. Miss Scarlett went away soon, and other folks came. The tutor, Hunt, was pleasant and nice. We left at 10.30. (Bitter cold and sleet.) Baring and I sat up late till 11.30. Charles Blunt of Salonica is dead![20]

Same strange weather: gray, and all cloudy-heavy, though not quite so bitter cold. Arranged packing till nine. Baring breakfasted at Mr Scarlett's. I alone. Then went out — dreary cold — and called on Mr Hill, leaving cards on General Church, old Campbell Johnston and Mr Scarlett. Returned at twelve, and had talk with Baring, and settled accounts. Lo! Andréa! the ancient man who took Franklin Lushington[21] and me through the Morea, and me to Tempe! — gave him a dollar cheerfully.

At 2.30 two carriages were packed, and I left Evelyn Baring, with regret. Wind less and rain beginning. At the Piraeus before four. Took places for Haniá. Went to 'Grand Bretagna' hotel, and later with George to the Kollas' — Spiro's brothers-in-law — and saw Mrs Spiro and little Amalía. Baring sent letters to post at Syra. At

25

5.20, having dined at the inn, came off: pouring rain, but I am consoled by the wind having fallen. At 6.30 we started in the *Oriente* once more. At eight, being intolerably sleepy, went to bed and slept more or less till eight next day: hard rain and little wind all night.

Rose at eight: and by nine was aboard the *Persia,* Austrian Lloyd for Haniá. Morning very clear and bright, but with gusts of fresh north wind. George and I went ashore and posted the two letters Baring had sent me, to Sir Henry Storks and to his brother. Then I went to a hotel *(Ὅλων Ἐθνῶν* — 'de toutes les nations') and breakfasted on lamb, beans and artichokes, very clean and civil. At ten George and I went up up up to the very top of the Roman Catholic 'Borgo', but without much joy: steps infinite, but views bounded on the north entirely.[22] At 12.30 we returned to the *Persia,* and are to go perhaps at midnight — sooner or later — and fifteen or sixteen hours to be our voyage.

(A queer analytic dryness of soul and mind and atmosphere seems to prevail at Athens and I don't know if it will do for life.)

Evil fortune! 350 or 400 pilgrims returning from the Madonna of Tinos are to embark;[23] half the upper deck is already full of them. Great row in separating men from women: one man and wife dismissed: *«Εἴμαι ἐλεύθερος — Ἕλληνας.»* ['I'm free — and a Greek.'] The *greco-orientale* from Smyrna is not yet in sight — 3.30 — and that is expected before the *celere,* so apparently we may be here till midnight. The second steamer came in about 5–5.30, but independent of delay in shipping freight and many more passengers, there was an awful row, four men having drawn knives, and one man was seized by the Captains and kept below till police came. Screams of the man's wife etc. etc. etc. were like a drama, and once or twice I thought worse would come of it. About nine the man was got off by policemen after great resistance, and later three other men were taken. At 10.30 we started. Went to bed, and the night being quiet — slept.

Morning fine, but wind increasing. Called by George at seven, up by eight, but could not stay on deck till after ten, when I lay down, only rising now and then all through the day. Crete in sight, but at 1 p.m. it is horridly rough, and a great sea on, with wind dead against us. It grew worse and worse and blew hard, though the *Persia* pitched only and rolled but little, and so on, till at five we entered the port of Haniá. But the beautiful approach to the Island of course I did not see, as it was hidden in cloud and, latterly, heavy rain. The 160 or 200 women and children all vomiting and wet through were a sight to see! Port is very picturesque, Pasha's Palace, etc. etc. but the boats! and crowd! At last the *καφιγί* [doorman] having recommended a black man, George and I and the eleven objects got on shore. No trouble with luggage etc. But the *Hotel* ('Constantinople') — *what* a place! A most filthy and wretched hole, and impossible to stay in. But the Pasha was away and the Consul lives some miles off; so all I could do was to send off my letter to him, and hope. Presently a young merchant, Guarracino

Haniá, 4.30 p.m., 26 May.

(Dutch Consul), called and became a good Samaritan by offering me his house, a bachelor's room only, which I gladly accepted. The English Vice-Consul [[Mr Boone]] also called, and I sent out my letter to Mr Hay:[24] also Elizabeth of Crete's[25] brother called. So I then set out with my new friend, and was soon at a tiny little house, where I was cordially welcomed, and installed in a room — my host's sitting room — many carpets etc. around. Soon came George with the *roba* [baggage] and, Mr Guarracino going out, I washed and George put up the camp bed. At eight came dinner: good macaroni, fish, and veal, olives and good cheese and wine. A Frenchman, Dr Baume, came who had known Pashley: Maniás [[Pashley's guide]] is dead. These people say I can go *anywhere* in safety. 10.15, bed; George has, I fear, rough quarters. So goes on my beginnings in Crete.

Rose at 6.30, having slept tolerably. George put up my bed, and we got out the 'Coliseum' [[a sack so called]] in hopes to draw: but it soon clouded and threatened rain. At 8.30 Mr Guarracino walked with me to the ramparts, I hoping to get a view from the walls, but it began to rain hard and nothing could be done. I see, however,

TUESDAY
12 APRIL

HANIA

27

that the Port is immensely picturesque. After the rain stopped and Mr Guarracino left me, George and I went through the bazaars — picturesque and crowdy — and 'out of the town'. Being shut up in high walls it is very invisible, but there must be some good views from the ramparts. We went out to a little height, and saw the village of Halépa, and the great White Mountains, half hidden in mist. Then towards a cemetery, where cypress and pine gleamed against far snow hills: and later, towards the west, but it rained hard, and we had to stand up, and at last came on to the city by 9.30, and, Petros (Mr Guarracino's servant) being out, we had to wait opposite the house till 10.30. The Cretans are vastly picturesque: great number of blacks, male and female.

4.30. I waited ready until twelve, when Mr Guarracino's breakfast took place: not very good, but heartily given. At one, he went out with George and me, taking us round the harbour by the lower gate and the great galley arches of the Venetians, and then George and I went on, as the rain had cleared off, by the shore towards Halépa, a village massed on the hill slopes two miles east of Haniá: and very like parts of Beirut, as to yellow or white flat-roofed houses, gardens, etc. etc. On the way are several fine views of Haniá, rocky and broad; and the queer village of the blacks, with houses in a cluster, was pretty. At Halépa I went to Mr Dendrino's with Paramythiótti's[26] letter: a large house with many kavasses and much pomp. I fought off dinner tomorrow, and went next to Drummond Hay's, who is a very nice fellow, losing, I fear, one eye by ophthalmia. His little girl and lovely Spanish wife were beautiful and interesting, and he also offered me a room. Looked at the country 'box' of Mr Guarracino, brought away some curry powder, and went up the hill some way, and then back by the shore; but it was far too windy to draw, so we walked by the cemetery and beheld the plain of Riza and its villages, and also the Sphakian mountains; though their tops are hidden, still a noble sight. Returned by six: how cold! Dinner not till eight: curry and hare, and one Petritini (nephew of Marcoran's,[27] cousin of Padovan[28]) sitting a long while — a bore — a greater his flea-full dog. The dogs are all timid, amicable and curly-tailed here. Bed — bored — by 9.45.

Scarcely any sleep. Wind, and the slamming window, and fleas uncountable from the Dog of last night. Rose before six, and came out with George, who slept worse but was ready. As we go out of the town we agree to buy various food and set off tomorrow to Halépa. I say I almost would go back to Athens, so disheartened I feel; but good George says laughing that would not do after so much bother and expense. Sitting by the roadside, overlooking the Riza, I drew till nearly nine. Picturesque peasants pass ever, and a few stop, but all are polite: the plain and hills greatly resemble Sparta. Weather seems improved, and the vast White Mountains partially gleam out, much like Olympus at times. But the wind makes drawing nearly impossible, and the *cold* is very disagreeable. We then went east of the city, and I drew Akrotíri in a small sketch: the colour of the ground and hills is singularly Palermitan — so red and russet yellow. Next we walked west of the city but saw little, for it began to rain: only lepers are there by the wayside. We got *home* — O! those Turkish pavements![29] — by eleven. I feel altogether out of heart, and looking at a stray sketch with Análipsis[30] on it, could cry for vexation that I can never walk there again: a pang as of exile, twinges me. George however, like a good man as he is, makes the best of all, and says truly, what should we have done but for this little room? It rains hard again, and Mr Guarracino enters. Noon.

Breakfast short, a ship of Mr Guarracino's having come, also a dog. He went, and it poured *torrents* all the rest of the day, and was bitterly cold. At seven he returned to dinner, after which Mr Petritini and another called, but I desired to rest.

Notes 5.30 p.m. It has rained cats and dogs all the afternoon; Mr Guarracino and I breakfasted, but he went out very shortly afterwards, a ship he had expected having come. *How* it rains! George was only able to get out to buy a Zante quilt and mattress, which I desired him to get for himself: but could get no eatables. As for me I read Pashley and later *Vanity Fair,* till 6 or 6.30, and it grew darker and colder — O! how cold! 7.30 dinner; Guarracino is really a hearty brick, and as George says, 'What could we have done without him?' Mr Petritini and another came in, but conversation rather induced than kept off sleep.

Haniá, 11 a.m., 14 April.

Rose at six. Bright sunshine and clear cold. At eight, leaving George to arrange about baggage, came out with Mr Guarracino, who took me good-naturedly round the ramparts. The range of White Mountains were wondrous, contrasted with the deep velvet green-gray of the hills and green of the plain. The city of Haniá has little inside worth drawing. Went out alone at 9.30, and drew on my yesterday's spot till ten. No-one molested me: two Turkish soldiers (one a black) came and said 'bono' and offered me a cigar. After which (going across by the Benghazi colony) I drew on the road to Halépa till 11.30. George passed me, with the *roba.* At twelve I was at Mr

Guarracino's house: a little room, swept out by George — comfortable. At 12.45 went to Consul Hay's, and dined at one: very pleasant and nice. Played and sung afterwards. At 3.30 Mrs Hay riding a pony, Mr Hay and I and a kavass and two dogs, went up the hill towards Akrotíri. Very fine views of Haniá. Stony roads — so called — as bad as those in Cerigo. Beyond summit, wonderful view of Suda Bay, and Mount Ida beyond. I never saw anything finer or lovelier. We returned by a lower path by 6.30. At seven went in to the Hays; Mr Guarracino came. Played and sung, and wrote out some Tennyson songs,[31] and came away to bed at 9.30–10.

FRIDAY 15 APRIL

HALEPA AKROTIRI HALEPA

Rose at five, having slept tolerably, barring a dog barking about level with my ear. Took the Políti medicine — Magnesia — for I have not been well for some days. And having spent three hours in dividing paper and clothes for travel, George and I started at eight — up to the hills. But it was a cloudy morning, and chilly. We pass the ugly arch and up-passage, and the fifty-dog piazza (the dogs, however, never bark or look at us, and are wholly silent unless other dogs appear) and go by the narrow lane (where banks and walls have fallen — 'feriti' [damaged] as George says, by the σεισμός [earthquake] of 1856, and upset by heavy rains) to the end of the olives, rising ever on the hillside. Here I drew, from 8.30 to 10, a needful drawing to understand the anatomy of the town etc., in an east light. But the view sadly wants good lines and balance, and can only be made good by sunset and clouds. Then we went on, across to Akrotíri isthmus, to the wondrous Suda Bay view, where Ida — if indeed it be Ida — was clear and splendid, though all the rest was purple cold. Drew till 12.30, and then went to rocks opposite the end of Suda Bay (Maláxa hills) where I lunched on eggs, oranges and wine — pleasantly, and somewhat reminding me of old days but that a cold (healthy) wind disturbed me somewhat. George, patient and quiet, is always the same: a curiously philosophic man, and in his ways and intentions a gentleman in all respects. Sitting in the thyme and cistus, I drew two or three other bits, and towards three began to move downwards, over to werry werry hard hard rox which this Akrotíri is compogcd of. Cheerful clear bright air, but chilly . . . and so to the downhill sunset view, where I drew again till six. (It sadly wants interest and fullness.) Home (to Guarracino's house — he left for the town this morning) by 6.30. (The little room is very comfortable, only the rats and mice rush about horridly — 9 p.m.) After a wash, went to Drummond Hay's, whose house reminds me of Cairo: he and his wife and child are interesting to a great amount, and he is also a well informed and superior man, if I know anything. He recounts how I am already called the Queen of England's doctor; and how the Pasha comes tomorrow; and how it is probable he may not like anyone to go into Sphakiá;[32] and how Guarracino has absurdly quarrelled with said Pasha Ismail on a ridiculous point of etiquette. So small are human fiddledibobberies. At 7.30 I left the Πρόξενος [Consul] and came across; George had got me a dinner of roast lamb and boiled artichokes, which with coffee made a good 'repast'. Wine ἔτσι κ' ἔτσι [so-so]. At nine ἔγραψα τοῦτο, καὶ θέλω νὰ κοιμηθῶ [I wrote this, and want to go to sleep].

30

Haniá (a painting based on a drawing made on 15 April).

I much doubt Crete being a *picturesque* country in any way, or that it will repay much trouble in seeing it. Its antiquities etc. *so* old as to be all but invisible; its buildings, monasteries, etc. nil; its Turkish towns fourth-rate. Rats O! and gnats.

Notes 15th April. The view of Haniá is very expressive and characteristic of this place, which is spread out before one: but it wants certain qualities of distant form which can't be given, and only sunset and clouds can make it compose well. When the morning sun shines on it the upper part — all white — and the Blacks' village by the shore look exactly like Syrian places; the long red line of wall being between the two.

The Suda Bay view is very Sicilian in its variety of isolate form, but bluer — grayer — 'Claudier'; though it is not unlike the colour about Hybla Megaris [in Sicily].

Little sleep: rats, nats, cats, bats; and toward morning a hurricane of wind and pouring rain again! So I lay in bed till eight. The good-natured Drummond Hay called. At ten went there — not over well — and copied Captain Spratt's map and played with Madeleine and on the piano till one, when we dined very pleasantly. Music and talk till five, when Mr and Mrs Hay rode out, and I walked with George a little way, down to Haniá road and up by another way to the village, by rocky wall-girt lanes, where cactus and aloes abounded. Windy and cloudy.

Came home and went to the Drummond Hays' and stayed there till 9.30.

Mr Dendrino invites for dinner tomorrow. Ismail Pasha has returned.

The rain stopped only about 3 p.m.

Petros was busy this morning with twenty little chickens just hatched, *oiling* their bills and backsides; for, said he, *«Ἄν δὲν κάμω τοῦτο, δὲν ἐμποροῦν νὰ τρώγουν ποτέ, μήτε νὰ κατουρήσουν!»* ['If I don't do this, they won't ever be able to eat or pee!']

Perfectly lovely: rose at 5.30, and at 6.30 out with George to the rox halfway to Haniá, where I drew from 7 to 8.30, and later from 8.30 to 9; after which I drew the Akrotíri promontery and the sandy foreground, where dogs and crows abound [[keeping watch on the treasures of the Haniá slaughter houses, which are on the beach below, as are also some bathing houses of the Pasha]]. The Cretans are incurious, and hardly

ever look at me when working, though they often say *«ἀντίο»* ['good-bye'] or *«ὥρα καλή»* ['good day']. Similarly act the dogs, who don't bark, except at other dogs: a tall thin cowardly race. Those of the Arabs' and Blacks' villages fight in troops. Morning lovely — plashy sea and Hastings memories. Plymouth memories also! ahi.[33] Consul Hay passed, on a visit to Ismail Pasha, and I returned home and put on a black coat and gray 'pants'. At 11.15 Mr Hay returned. Ismail Pasha is in good humour, and protests every wish to help me in every way. He is to stop two things: the abduction of girls, and the demonstrations of Turks if any of them is killed by Greeks.

At 11.30 set out again with George: a pleasant walk till the horrid Turkey pavement was reached. The Pasha's palace: all grandiose and dirty below, good rooms above. Lots of men — room empty — some oranges on one table and oysters on another. Guards usher in Pasha: short and stout, intelligent and governorish. Offered to take me with him to Rethymnon: I demurred; to let me have guards — guides — *«ὅπως θέλω»* ['as I wish']. Speaks French. *Chibouque* and *café*. Came M. Michel,[34] the architect of lighthouses, and some beys, and a Greek bishop. Bored out of my life, having got a sudden deafness from cold. Came away soon, and got to Halépa by 1.30. Wrote and read till 2.30, and then went to Dendrino, the Russian Consul: large and empty house; dinner friendly plain. Society distinctly a dreadful bore, all but old Dendrino himself who is well bred, cheerful and pleasant. Madame Leonidoff [[the wife of a Russian secretary]] was ugly and very coarse, and spoke Russian only. Guarracino cross and disagreeable. I disagreeable.

32

George Kokáli
(said to be by Lear).

Society flagged and broke up at five, when I went down to the rocks with George and drew till 6.30, and at seven went to the Hays' to tea and sat till 9.30.

MONDAY
18 APRIL

HALEPA
NEROKOUROU
MOURNIES
PERIVOLIA
KATSISTROHORI
HALEPA

Rose at five. For two days I have been bothered with deafness in my left ear, result of cold partly, part[ly] of stomach. Set off at six with George — morning truly lovely — by the Arab huts to the Rethymnon road, the way enlivened by a 'mule-making', as at Samos ineffectual.[35] Surely if all mules — and they are legion — are so made, it is a difficult art. Having no particular plan, I left the road and struck off towards the hills, leaving Hrysopighí to the right: apparently a church only, with ruined walls around. The plain here is little cultivated, and as one goes on, the olives (however fruitful) are scrubby and ugly. Closer lanes and more cultivation, and rising ground, brought one up to a village — mostly ruined in the outskirts — whence was a good view of Suda Bay, which I sat to draw. A little (Turkey) girl [[with fez and large trousers]] came and talked. Nerokoúrou — or Nerokírou — they seem to call the village — or Meropoúli. But no-one came to look at or bother one, and I can't remember any day more free from bore in any country. Only two men called out, later in the day as I went up a hillside, 'That road leads to no village.' 'Teach me the tongue you speak', said the girl; and to George 'Why don't you draw?' ('Don't you see, I am too short?' was one of George's queer answers.)

About nine we went on, always above the plain, skirting the mountain bases: what ruined houses — walls — churches! Yet, very tiny churches are still abundant.

33

We tried many short cuts, but unforeseen ravines made us haste back. Asphodels and squills covered the ground, with thousands of flowers, and about 10.30 we came to a spot where vast lots of that brutal-filthy yet picturesque plant grew: the black arum, which first I recollect to have seen at Marathon, in 1848. All the plain of Haniá is grand, as far as food goes, but unavailable for drawing: the long flat tubular line of Akrotíri alone — and hardly — relieves it. Walking on, about Mourniés, the olives grow finer, and there is a richer vegetation of gardenism. Birds are plentiful: ravens, hooded crows, orioles, bee-eaters and hoopoes. At twelve we reach a high olive tree, and sit in its shade to lunch: eggs, wine, lamb and bread and oranges. No dogs — no nothing — no annoyances. For a while I think the same hills, flowers, sounds, tastes, etc. . . . are here as about the Tivoli hills in 1837; so strange and dreamlike is life, it seems to me. In vain I try to draw hence; the few dry olives forbid. We walk on. Ever small ruined churches, and here and there one not ruined. But there is no intoxication of beauty here, as at Damascus, Palermo, etc. (Cistus and *fern* abound.) At two I draw above a ruined monastery, over gulfs of fern and underwood, looking, beyond great olives and lemon groves, to the plain and city. Thence we still went west, till it was time to strike back, and so we crossed deep dells *full* of 'lemon groves', most remarkable in extent and richness. The olives here too were older and larger than heretofore, and one or two drawings ought to be made here — Perivólia. In the villages we passed the very few villagers we saw never moved, but said «καλῶς ὡρίσατε» ['welcome'] as if they saw strangers daily. Greater olives make lovelier scenes, and we pass Katsistrohóri and get into great cornfields, with the snow hills beyond the dark olives. (A Turkish farm, the inmates unlike the Greeks: woolly-headed children playing.) Passing two or three villages, and fearing to draw lest time should fail, we walked on, and got to Halépa by six. A charming day, and calm. Arrived at the village, I find I am asked to dine tomorrow at Ismail Pasha's; a sad bore. ᾿Αλλά τί νὰ κάμω; [But what can I do?] Went to the Hays' for an hour, and then returned to dine well, and to write this.

TUESDAY
19 APRIL

HALEPA
HANIA
HALEPA

Stoppage in boles, and unwell. Took lots of medicine, yet was able to walk out by seven, when I drew on the road by the rox till eight, and then, entering the town, in a café gallery till 9.30. Wonderfully incurious people are these. Next, went to Consul Hay's office, where Mr Henry Moazza (a Cerigotto merchant) met me. He knows every part of Crete, and is able to give me letters anywhere. My plan is to do the Akrotíri this week, and the west coast on the following; then going to Megalókastro [Herákleion] with Mr Hay, and thenceforward as may be most convenient. Moazza seems a very good fellow. Then after that I went to see Guarracino and asking about the view of the port, a Bey volunteered to take me to a *casino* [[or club]], and did so; but he was a fearful bore. At one we came — George and I — away from that 'sweet city',[36] and now I have been lunching, while Ismail Pasha is paying a visit to the Consul and the courtyard is full of kavasses and grooms and officers, all a-diverting of themselves with the monkey. It is 2.30 p.m.

Haniá, 9 a.m., 19 April.

At 3.30 sat with the Hays, and walked on the terrace, till I dressed, and at 5.30 walked with Consul Hay — O! bother the pavement! — to the Pasha's. Dinner at seven, all in the European style. Twenty dishes, and only one wine. Pasha not conversible, and talking in Turkish to t'other cove [Azif Pasha, Governor of Rethymnon]. Afterwards, pipes and coffee, a Greek bishop and a Greek dragoman, whom Ismail Pasha snubbed. Elizabeth of Crete [[in a brown gown and velvet bonnet]] passed us as we went in: did I write about her debt of £400 to Hill? We left at 9.45, accompanied beyond the gate by two lantern-bearers. [[It was thought best that I should apply to the Pasha for one of his men to act as guide in my journeys about the island: not, according to all, that any guard is wanted; but were I to decline an escort of government I might be supposed to have anti-Turkish designs, and secret communications with the disaffected — of which there are no lack. On the other hand the presence of a Mussulman guard will cause a certain restraint in Cretan Christian families; but as to refuse would create suspicion, I acquiesce.]] A man is set apart to accompany me, and if possible I shall get off on Thursday. Moonlight, and walk home by 10.30 pretty well tired.

At 6.30 walked to 'town' with George and to the Consulate, having first drawn a little near the gate — no easy matter, for the crowds. Sent for my travelling kavass and for someone to go on the walls. The former, named Zeriff — or Zareef —, does not seem to like the idea of walking much. The latter, with a sergeant, accompanied me to the walls where I drew the mountains, and after that — plague on this tumbling in Turkish paved streets! — we came up to Halépa at 10.30 or 11. The troops, as we went, were exercising and their music is amazing queer and shrieky-dissonant. Lunched at twelve, and then sat with the Hays, and when they went out on horseback began to make an Alphabet for little Madeleine. At six, dinner: George giving me stewed lamb and beans. Great difficulty in arranging *roba* for tomorrow. Sat with the Hays till 9.30, playing and singing, etc. The little girl is a wonderfully interesting child.

To leave *roba* here — at Guarracino's — or not? George says yes: 'disprezzo sarebbe di mandasta vai' ['it would be an insult to go'] and perhaps, as for two days, better so. The bother is — how to take enough in a small compass? 11 a.m. lunch: fresh air, beautiful dark sea, orange red earth and flat-roofed, white-topped houses. Guarracino's courtyard: geese, fowls, guinea-hens, turkeys, great pigeons, dux, almond trees.

For in all ages the Priest has been the advocate of lying, the promoter of darkness and hatred, the antagonist of light and progress: and enduring and [?gross] as his injuries to his fellow men have ever been, yet he has worked them with impunity, knowing himself to be safe under the never-failing shields of superstition and fanaticism. Nor are the propensities of the Priesthood as a body one whit changed or mitigated even in our own day, save by the only safeguard of nations — law and reason: were these restraints removed, a Cullen, a Cumming, or a Denison, each a type of the foul and bitter spirit of the concrete priest, would gladly forego their mutual hatred for a time, if for one hour they could join in a howl and dance of joy round a pile which should consume a Jowett, a Stanley or a Williams.[37]

THURSDAY
21 APRIL

HALEPA
AGHIA TRIADHA
AGHIOS IOANNIS
KATHOLIKO
AGHIOS IOANNIS
AGHIA TRIADHA

As I expected from the sunset, all is cloud. Verily, this Cretan journey prospereth not. Boles all wrong. Saw Guarracino at six, rising, with Petritini in another room. Poor George had even less sleep than I, from dogs and other ἐμποδίσματα [obstacles]. Zeriff, with his horse, was ready at five. Taking but little *roba* we set out — for of what use is it to wait for fine weather? [[And what consolation is it to hear that such late rains were never known before as are in Crete this year? — much as we English tell foreigners that east winds and bitter cold in June, long dreary rains through July and August, and fogs in September are 'quite extraordinary and never occurred before the present year'.]] As we go up the stony paths of Akrotíri there would be a magnificent view, but nothing is clear. The same hard stones, the same thyme, cistus, lavender and thorny euphorbia abound. Long undulating lines succeed each other, but all distance is shut out, and at nine (we started at 6.45) the rain begins. Oleanders, and the black arum, and squills. We go near villages and there are numbers of olives. It rains hard and is very cold as we near Aghia Triádha, where we arrive at 9.45 — just three hours' walk. The monastery is picturesque, and the *Hegoúmenos* [Abbot] (Gregórios) is polite and pleasant: coffee and sweets as usual, and soon a dish of eggs, olives, caviare and *astonishing* wine! At eleven it had cleared more or less, and I and Zeriff and George set out to see the other convent. A rapid rise of the usual stones and herbs led to a wild and narrow pass below great heights of crags — but my boles caused me to stop continually on the way up — reaching Aghios Ioánnis at 12.10. Here we took a Cretan, white-cloaked, to show us the way, and in half an hour by a bad path reached Katholikó: in a most dreary dreadful depth, a ruined hermitage or monastery which must have been of greater importance than its size proclaims [in view of] the great flight of steps and the vast bridge below. Most gloomy scene! But I could hardly begin to draw it when the rain came, and drove us upward to Aghios Ioánnis. Here we waited, arriving at one, till three; thunder and rain meanwhile. An old *Hegoúmenos* was kindly polite. It was impossible to draw, so, setting out at four, we went down to the monastery again. All the evening has gone in talking with *Hegoúmenos* Gregórios. It would not have been possible anyhow to have made anything out of Aghios Ioánnis — a mere wall and white dome — but it must be said nonetheless that fortune attendeth not this *giro*. The pleasant yet not servile manners of these people are very nice. The morning meal of Gregórios was bean soup, olives, and snails: of which last he seemed ashamed, asking if we in England ate them? I consoling him with the fact of periwinkles (κοχλίες τῆς θάλασσας) [sea snails] being so. In the evening there were bits of kid roast for me, and a good pilaf, with a large glass of the most superb wine I ever tasted. Gregory was free on the subject of fasts, and is in fact a 'Protestant' against all but what he thinks original dogmas of the church. Asking about Pashley, I find that he [Gregórios] is a Sphakiot of [[Kallikráti]], and that Maniás's daughter has married his brother. When Zeriff enters Sphakiot subjects are shelved: [[the very sound of the name seems to import rebellion to the Turkish authority, and is tabooed accordingly]]. I was a good deal worn out with constant diarrhoea, and felt cold, but passed the evening very pleasantly. The large refectory is like a schoolroom in England. Later I went to his own room, where he has lots of books: lexicons, etc. etc. Then was shown mine: a room over the refectory, eight-windowed, clean and with a good bed.

Slept perfectly (not one flea!) till a bell sounded, and dog accompanist. At 5.30 rose. It is fine, and the yellowgreen sunlight is pleasant on the vines and fig trees in the meadowland beyond the monastery, and the fields of olive trees. Beyond, the Sphakiot mountains are nearly clear, though gray. I am better this morning. Gregórios Petrídhis and Ieramías Bernardhákis gave me coffee (Kallikráti is the former's home) and took me to see the church etc. The church is *very* simple: red and white, and but few pictures. Also I saw a *taphos* [tomb] of the original builder, and a closet full of bones. At seven, leaving this well-bred and intelligent *Hegoúmenos*, we set out. From

FRIDAY
22 APRIL

AGHIA TRIADHA
HALEPA

below the monastery a slender drawing may be made, but of very little importance: scantily little in this land is there to draw; its stunted harsh small olives, and its ever stony surface. I begin to think Crete is a 'sell'. However, I drew once or twice more before 10.30, when we reached the spot looking over the bay and Haniá; and, as the weather is lovely, so there is a certain charm in the view — but it is wide and flabby and rich. Here we lunched. Zeriff is vastly quiet and sad, and by no means a help to 'society'; however he is obedient and good.

Drew till 1 p.m. Alas! for Crete, it seems a sell; and when I think of Sicily and its every step and every moment of interest, while here is so little, except that of floral nature and the delight of the sweet morning air and thorough calm. George always enjoys himself in the hours when I am busy, wandering or poking about flowers or insects, or observing the ways of the people, or sitting still: never in, nor out of, the way;[38] a real good man. However, ἐπειδή εἶναι ἀνάγκη ὅτι κάμωμε τὴν Κρήτη, ἄς τὴν κάμωμε καλά [since it's necessary to 'do' Crete, let's do it well].

We reached Halépa at 1.30. The Consul, I hear, has just set off to Aghia Triádha. I set to work 'arranging' this scrap of a room, while George has gone to 'town' for some meat. Few peasants we passed or met today, but all salute kindly. Black arum abounds in patches. Let us not compare Crete with Sicily!

'Cleaned myself', read, wrote and walked about for two or three hours observing the filth of the courtyard below, in which there are nine sorts of creatures: goat, dog, cat, goose, duck, turkey, guinea-fowl, fowls and pigeons. The odour and fleas from these! How George goes on at all I cannot tell. Watched the little Madeleine and the little Maltese girl in the courtyard with the Arab servant [Hassan Eyn] and the monkey, and later, at 5.30, went to the Consulate where I did somewhat to Madeleine's alphabet and played and sang to her, a very remarkably sweet little child. I wonder where Mary De Vere is? Queer blank spaces of life! At six (George being at home) I find Consul Hay and Mrs Hay return from Aghia Triádha; their admiration of all that is beautiful in scenery is very refreshing. Not over well (and having strained my left wrist), I did not stay long in the Consul's house, but inwardly resolved to go there altogether on Sunday. At 7.30 poor George gave me a dinner of pilaf and stewed artichokes, but how he can cook or arrange anything, as things are below, I can't tell. Bed at 9.30. Did I note that I had seen the death of kind good Miss Duckworth?[39] Read *Villette*.

Perivólia (of Rethymnon),
2 p.m., 3 May.

Rose at five. Very lovely, and George and I off at six; I in great pain from some
unknown cause in left foot — left wrist also very painful. Out of spirits. Hobbled to the
streets by the gate and drew a little, so that now I can make a drawing of it. Then by
the paved Turkish road, drawing a picturesque tomb, towards the Perivólia villages.
Drew below a large olive — at this part of the plain there are really fine trees — the
beautiful scene I had marked on the [18th]: foreground a great waving pale green corn
meadow, then large olives deep gray beneath the green down-like hills, topped by the
snow range. Beyond this, at nine, we threaded through ruined villages — what a state
they are in! — hardly seeing a soul, to the west of the plain; but then, missing our way,
had to work back till we reached the huge olive boles, whence all the plain is seen, a
blaze of colour: the yellow-green of the plain and the frittery bright lemon groves, the

39

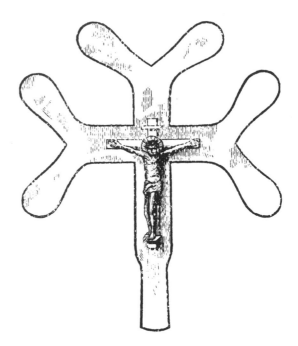

The crucifix of Aghios Elevthérios
(from Tozer's *Islands of the Aegean*).

darker orange, gray olive, red cliffs, lilac hills and blue sea! Nightingales delighted by singing, orioles and hoopoes by showing themselves. Nor were we molested, once only being spoken to by a suspicious Turk: «Λεμόνια γράφεις; κι' διατί λεμόνια;» ['Are you drawing lemons? and why lemons?'] [[reminding me of Signor [Rivettini at Gioiosa] in Calabria who said 'Perchè?' on all occasions]]. Certainly this corner of the plain of Haniá is wonderfully lovely, and the lemon groves are positively amazing. We began about eleven to wind below the hills toward Mourniés, meeting three leprous men on horseback. The hedges hereabouts are full of most *enormous* aloes, and the ground one sheet of rosy cistus bloom. At twelve we lunched, just below where we lunched on the [18th] and not far from the monastery of Harodhiá. But everything, except nature, is in ruin here. At 12.30 we go on and turn to the village of Mourniés, a long street and very considerable village, though hidden — so low are its houses — by the olives on the plain. Not far beyond this is Aghios Elevthérios, where, as Pashley says, there is a carved crucifix; but the foolish *Hegoúmenos* assured me all Greek churches had such.[40] Thus we made across the plain till we reached the Rethymnon road, and arrived at Halépa by 3.30. George is, and no wonder, put out that Petros has sent no meat nor vegetables as he promised; but I can't let George go to town again, so must dine on pilaf. Health better than when I started.

Dined as above, and sat afterwards with the Hays till nine. Night bad, from vermin and from noise; Guarracino and his friends coming in at one or two after midnight, dogs, etc. etc.

Wonderful beauty of Perivólia gardens! Lemon, orange, plane, vine, pomegranate. Hedges [?about] — *vast* aloes — myrtle and sheets of cistus. Olives very large. Three lepers. Asphodels.

40

Fine all day — till four or five, when heavy clouds arose. Having packed up all, told Guarracino I was going to the Consul's. Wrote to Chichester Fortescue,[41] Franklin Lushington, Ellen, and Evelyn Baring. Sent George to town for quinine. At twelve, went to Mr Hay's and dined with them at 1.30. At 3.30 walked with them, little Madeleine, the kavass and Hassan Eyn nearly to the town, returning by rocky upper paths by six. Called on Mr Dendrino — out. All my things are up at the Consul's, in the nicest pleasantest room possible. Sat, and tea, till nine with Mr and Mrs Hay, then bed. The gloom and wind seem once more to forbid the morrow's journey.

George called me at five, but from two or three it had blown a gale and clouds and rain and tempest prevailed. 'Was there ever such a climate?' So I rose at six and at seven or eight, having seen the 'family', came during their breakfast to work at little Madeleine's letters. Went over accounts also with George; and so till ten. Zeriff has been, but sent away. There can be no starting today. Meanwhile I finish the alphabet, and am literally *shivering* with cold. Violent wind and roaring sea all day. George and I went down to the Arab sands about four or five and I drew a little, but my foot is still bad, though my hand is better. Depressed and restless it is I am. Came back, and tea and talk at evening with the Hays. Papers: Chichester Fortescue is a Privy Councillor — Rt Hon. C. F.

Fine. Slept well, having scalded my 'poor feet'; but whether the malady is corn or thorn — know not. We are ready, but no Zeriff has yet appeared though it is 6.30: a bore. He comes at 7.10, and at 7.30 we are off. His horse seems good and lively [[and carries my bed and George's as well as saddlebags of clothes and drawing materials]]. Pass the city and the odious paved road by the gate. The lepers in their villages, great aloes, lupins, somewhat Sicilian ever. Asphodel in bloom in patches. Theatre-like coombs. Village — or buildings — on high ground on the right: Makrý Teihos. Leper woman beggar. Timid but civil peasants.

9.30 The seashore fronting Aghios Theódhoros: sand, rox, great foaming sea. Akrotíri afar; shadowy White Mountains above nearer sandy green slope. 10.15 Corner of Aghios Theódhoros turned: promontery of Aghia Marína. Lovely breezy morning. Stop to draw: and lo, the village I thought Aghia Marína is Platanía, on a hill. 10.20 Stop to draw till eleven and then pass it, making for *the* trees[42] and the river, which we reach by twelve along refreshing nightingale-haunted green lanes. But alas! Platanía is χαλασμένη [ruined]! The death of the vines [[by the vine disease two years ago]] made the plane trees useless, and all are cut down but a very few and, barring the snow heights, the river scene might be in Epirus or anywhere. At one I have lunched on cold fowl and wine, lying on the goatshair baggage-cover with my cloak as a cushion, a world of green and yellow in front — grass and buttercups — and over them two or three vast planes. The ἀηδόνια [nightingales] are stupendous and delight me and George. Zeriff hubblebubbles, and is composed. Air delightful, also the trickle of streams; 'amaranth and moly'.[43] Bee-eaters, wrens, titmice, severally agreeable.

TUESDAY
26 APRIL

HALEPA
MAKRY TEIHOS
AGHIA MARINA
PLATANIA
MONASTERY OF
GHONIA

Plataniá, 11 a.m., 26 April.

Variety of nightingale's notes! George says, *«Πρέπει νά ἔχη περισσότερα μυαλά παρά τὰ ἄλλα πουλιά [[διότι δὲν τραγουδάει ποτέ δύο φορές τὸ ἴδιο]].»* ['It must have more brains than other birds because it never sings the same thing twice.'] Come two men [[valuable for their services as 'figures' in Cretan costume]], saying we eat and spoil their grass; so we prepare to go. Pass the first small river and second larger, but not deep, on an 'oss and an ass. At 2 p.m. take right side of river: corn and olives, sunshine and glades, sheep and goats. Descend, but not to sea; stony road parallel. Poverty of outline! Lean and meagre length! Cross several streamlets, oleander-grown, in more or less deep hollows which look ominous of malaria in summertime.

3 p.m. Same route, nearer shore: corn and low hills; White Mountains beyond; the long bay and promontery of Dictynnaeum in front: but *nothing drawable*, and so on — so on — so on — till four. Green silly plain fields, and here and there asphodels in full bloom! I half resolve to return to Haniá tomorrow. Ever the plain; two other streams; two villages, mostly in ruins, at 4.30.

4.45 Few people; almost desert-like plain, but the monastery of Ghoniá ('in a corner') is fine in its way, and I draw it. Again, ascending to it, the view of the mountains is really beautiful: the black rocks, and breaking sea. Monastery picturesque-ish, but mostly church, and the priests are in it. Dark room, not promising. Wander alone above, and find the scene far finer than Schranz gives an idea of.[44] Return, and find *Hegoúmenos* and other filthy friars, but all hearty and speaking good Greek. Get some time alone and wash face, hands and feet and change sox, so am up to politeness. Translate Pashley to them, which pleases them, particularly about the Trieste pictures.[45] About seven a 'table' comes, with excellent rice and tomato pilaf, eggs and good cheese. The wine as usual is absolutely astonishing and not unlike a light port. The *Hegoúmenos* would smoke a *nargileh*, [for] which the young attendant Narkódhios (*«διότι μεταλλάζονται ὅλα τὰ ὀνόματά μας»*

Ghoniá, 5.30 p.m., 26 April.

['because all our names are changed']) ardently snubbed him, and indeed he is rather a bore. At length, at 8.45, I got the room clear, but George is still endeavouring to get a po — that unattainable article in Greek monasteries and houses. A long and queer day of Cretan travels. O fleas! Poor George has been obliged to eat νηστεύματα [Lenten food], the pilaf and eggs going to the Turk [[and the 'arriving voyager' as I once saw written on a placard at a German inn: after a long day's walk it is not a bad thing to be of the wrong religion in these places, and consequently beyond risk of starvation]].

Little sleep: fleas endless, spite of fleapowder — awful bore. Rose at 5.30; dressed, packed and coffee by 6.30. Morning gray, but calm and fine. After coffee, and the *Hegoúmenos* chanting to me about the Holy Taphos [Holy Sepulchre], went out above the monastery and drew till nearly eight; then below (escaping adieux, as I intend to return on Friday), about the rox till 8.25. George, Zeriff and horse join me, and we are off by 8.30. The Ghoniá scene is the best I have come upon in Crete yet. We keep east of the hills below Ghribiliana — corn and olives ever — and then move westward. Warm though sunless. Thick beautiful olive dells (the trees however in themselves not large) recall Girgenti, but the hills are roundy and not very drawable. 9.20 Ascent above the village of Spiliá: beautiful groves of olive! Ἀηδόνια [nightingales]. 9.25 Reach Pashley's fountain, but only one plane is left. Below are gardens of oranges and lemons and extremely lovely Corfu-like scenery. Great ascent: top, 9.45. Down again, and another [way] leads down to a shut-in plain: olives and a village. Thence another

WEDNESDAY
27 APRIL

MONASTERY OF
GHONIA
SPILIA
TA NOPIGHIA
DHRAPANIA
BADHOURIANA
KALOUDHIANA
TOPOLIA

43

long and tedious stony ascent, near the top of which I rest at 10.30. The few peasants I meet are all courteous. Doubt my getting beyond the Palaiókastro. 10.45 Valleys, and the plain of Kissamos. 10.55 We stop at a fountain and eat bread and egg. At eleven I draw again, a gloomy and fine gorge above a smiling valley, but sunlight is absent. Later, in sight of the sea and of both capes, draw again. By this it was nearly twelve, and we were soon at the village of Ta Nopíghia. Zeriff would neither eat nor drink,

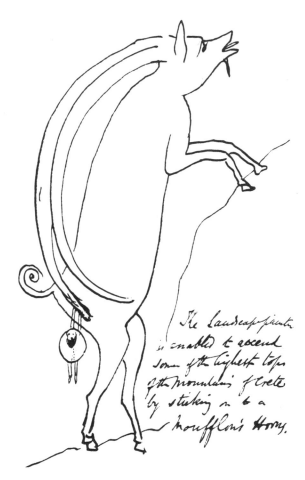

The landscape-painter is enabled to ascend some of the highest tops of the mountains of Crete by sticking on to a moufflon's horn.

and did not seem to like to unload, though we found that Kyrios Armenákis [[to whom Moazza had given me a letter]] lived at Topólia, and not here; and so we went on, though Topólia is said to be four hours off. A small river and women washing: an ὠφέλιμος γαΐδαρος [useful donkey] took over George and me. Fine thick olives and generally pleasant ways brought us to Dhrapaniá by one, and there we learned that a brother of Armenákis had gone to see me at Ghoniá. So we unloaded in a pothousy *khan*, and ate eggs and herrings and drank wine till two. Truly a pothouse, as innumerable little pots hang on high, and below — greater pots: on the 'dresser' some twenty or thirty *nargilehs*. George pays $4^{1}/_{2}$ piastres for our entertainment. We comment on the trousery women. Having left this Palazzo, I sit on a low wall; the

44

stony-centre-paved lane is bordered by a yard of dust on each side, then a foot of green, then the low wall — green, ox-eyes and poppies thereon, and olives beyond as far as sight can go. O! olives of Crete! oily, thick and fruitful as to produce, but dry, squat and humdrum to behold! O my Análipsis olives! Even yet I dare not think of those places.

2 p.m. Set off: long olive (Lefchimo-like) groves, only smaller trees, τρυγόνια [turtle-doves], aloes, pleasant villages (Badhourianá and Kaloudhianá), bothering river (the Typhlós); George and I cross barefoot. We continually, after 2.30, ascend a rather severe ridge, having on right and left deep great valleys wholly cultivated — olive, corn and mulberry — and sloping up to a great height: above them on the left, divided by I know not what deeps, are picturesque rocky heights, the whole often and vividly recalling Calabrian days. Now — 4.10 — we are almost at the end of the valley, its sides uniting in a vastly picturesque hollow. On the right, where we are, are ledges of cultivated ground and endless verdure of corn, olive and fruit trees, and I suppose Kyrios Armenákis's house — if house he hath — is thereabouts: anyhow it is a fine scene. (Yellow broom abounds.) Villages sparkle, but small and scattery, everywhere. Continual ascent, but a more beautiful valley and mountain scene can hardly be. It is most like Cánalo in Calabria, but that was more rocky and less cultivated on the hillsides. After another ascent we go down very low into the end of the valley and arrive at a low flat peasant house, no way externally differing from most of the others, and as I see they are sweeping and unbundling a room within, lo, I look for fleas and misery. Presently a fat brown man, Manouélis Armenákis, appears, and pleasing wife. They show me a good-sized, tolerably clean room: divans and bed. Discourse with Kyrios Armenákis till 5.30, having had coffee. We then go about the village, and one can hardly see any more picturesque and interesting. [[Mostly the peasants rose as we passed, and the greater number say «καλῶς ὡρίσατε» ['welcome'] or some similar greeting: one old woman however was very demonstrative and vociferous, blessing me loudly, and hailing me as a harbinger of liberty of which I knew nothing.]] Down to the Monastery of Aghia Triádha, my fat friend, who dresses anglika [English-style]-cum-fez, preceding me. All the people are most civil, and courteous. Return at 6.15; arranged drawings till 7.30. Large room, with a round table, looking glass and Louis Napoleon portrait. Shortly after, though I was nearly asleep, came Kyrios Armenákis, and afterwards supper, the prettyish wife waiting at table. [[She is a 'Turk', i.e., a Moslem Cretan.]] Dish of stewed artichokes and lamb, doves, cheese, olives, bottarga [dried smoked roe] and astonishing wine. Telling Kyrios Armenákis of Maniás, I regret I can't talk to him about Pashley as I could wish — the sort of way in which one has stuttered out bad Greek for two hours! Back 'returns the dark' etc.,[46] for I never seem to progress. George comes and says, «Κανέν πῶ θὰ εὑρίσκεται· τὶ νὰ κάμω;» ['No po is to be found; what am I to do?'] I incline to stay here tomorrow, and to go afterwards to Palaiókastro. 10.15 All things being quiet, I found the bed impossible, so had to unroll and 'fix' my own, as George was asleep. Also I seized on a tin wash basin for po.

Rose before six: sky cloudy and threatening. 6.45, after nutshell coffee, went down to the Aghia Triádha Monastery. Topólia contains 100 houses (500 souls), all flat-roofed, and low and box-like. Lane-streets nasty and rough, but once beyond the village the situation is delightful. Draw the chasm at the end of the valley till 7.30, and at eight, shower — heavy. Commence another drawing, and finish it by fits, between showers, at 9.20. Singing of nightingales is wonderful here: also turtles abound. Rain, but clears. Return to house at 9.45. Kyrios Manouél is not unlike B. H. Hunt,[47] if dirty, and gives me a lunch of artichokes in lemony-oil, wild asparagus, eggs, cheese and wine. Set off with George at 10.45, hoping to get some views on yesterday's route, but though I went till 12.15 downhill, the weather clouded, all the hills were blotted out, and rain came on. Worse, the nearer Topólia hills, which I could have taken when I went, are not visible now; so at three I 'sit on a wall', disgusted utterly. Tried vainly to finish a drawing, but at four it began to pour. George the patient therefore came back to me, and it now — five — rains harder than ever. Sometimes I think of giving up farther endeavours to see Crete, at least this N.W. corner of it, and go back to Ghoniá tomorrow. There is so little peculiarly characteristic in the landscape that I weary. After dark came these hospitable people's dinner: 1. lamb — roast in oil 2. vineleaves, full of rice and meat — in oil 3. roast doves — in oil 4. macaroni and chopped meat — in oil. Manouél Armenákis and I talked for two hours such Greek as may be, and I go to bed at 8.30, the faithful George having arranged my bed as usual. A brootle dog barx — I hope not for long. Owls. What to do tomorrow? Kastélli, or Ghoniá? It is horridly cold. Memo: send a photograph of myself to Manouél Armenákis, and a view of Cerigo to Henry Moazza.

FRIDAY
29 APRIL

TOPOLIA
AGHIOS
KYR IOANNIS
KALATHENES
PALAIOKASTRO
KISSAMOS
DHRAPANIA

It has rained all night, and rains still at six. Now — 6.45 — it seems to be clearing. How about rivers! I vote, though reluctantly, for total departure from Kissamos province and for leaving Palaiókastro and Phalasarna unseen for ever. (The river close to Nopíghia is called Nopighianós; that we forded below these hills Typhlós.) 7.30 The weather clears, and Kyrios Manouél Armenákis persuades me to go to Kastélli: he says truly the Nopíghia mountains will be very bad after such rain. Off at 7.45. Drew above the valley, and off at eight.

Down: villages, foliage, water (Tivoli-like), mud (difficult), village (Aghios Kyr Ioánnis, mulberries, «καλή σας ἡμέρα» ['good day to you'], peasant quiet and courtesy), fountains, planes, moss, walnuts, lovely nooks, fern, great plane and other fountain, large village (Kaláthenes — no-one asks anything, quiet dogs), wild flower like syringa ('astíraka'),[48] cypress, oleander, smell of fern. Delightful walk.

At nine, we are on the ridge, and go down then up a hollow mountain ridge; cultivation mainly ceased. 9.20 On the top of number two *salita* [ascent], and other mountains, rocky (and down-like lower down), appear: vast rocky mountainsides. Another deep dell beyond, and a height with two villages on its further side. This turns out to be [[Epáno and Kato]] Palaiókastro, so, though large and lumpy, I drew it. Descend to the gully at bottom, and ascend to village. Very courteous handsome

Near Kifsamos [Kissamos],
27 [29?] April.

men and women: two of the latter at a fountain — most beautiful. Old tower — see
Pashley — horrid ugly. 10.30 We halt, and drink water and eat, getting some tolerable
wine, a bottle for $3^1/_2$ piastres. The peasants are most amiable and gentlemanly:
perhaps 17 or 18 are round me, but I cannot imagine a finer or more agreeable lot.
Presently I and George went with one of them, up to the *kastro*,[49] but really there are
no walls to compare with Krani or Samos [in Cephalonia]; only bits here and there,
and much of a Roman or later date. And as all the distance is more or less blotted out
by cloud, and is not anyhow lovely, and I could do nothing, I came down again at
twelve. Gave $2^1/_2$ piastres to the *kastro* guide, and 5 to the Topólia guide, who both
declined and seemed to be surprised [[saying, «Διατί, Κύριε; Δέν χρειάζεται» ['Why,
sir? It's not necessary']]]: the former kissed my hand. A wild grave circle of hills
surround this place, which is remote and savage to see, yet neither woman nor child
showed any fear, though they never could have seen a traveller hardly. Few
inhabitants, but all rose as I passed, and said, «Καλή σας ἡμέρα.» ['Good morning to
you.'] I never saw such quiet nice people.

47

Palaiókastro, 2 p.m., 29 April.

Downhill: stony roads and very little interest in scenery. From 1 p.m. to 1.30 made what I could of the Palaiókastro sepulchres cut in rock. Plain and shabby little town of Kissamos. We go on and nothing particular brings us down to the same. The only good feature, the promontery near [Cape Vouxa], is all covered with cloud. We go on — 1.40 — draw on the plain till two, and get to the miserable little town by 2.40; at whose outskirts Manouél Armenákis meets me, with brother Theoháris and a lame Cerigot, one Nikolákis Dharmáros, to whose house, a very nasty shattery place not far off, I am taken. With best intentions Mr Dharmáros is a bore, and talks politics, of the Ionians, etc., in tiresome English. He was with Captain Spratt and Ongley.[50] The Turkish *mudir* [[commander of the citadel]] arrived on a visit: that fat person comes with a colonel and major and 'suite' and we 'sit and smile'[51] at each other. Mr Dharmáros proposes a visit to the Governor and to see some antiquities, so I go with him and Manouél Armenákis: a bore (except a glass of lemonade). Then, with a *cadi* [judge], it is necessary to go all over the fort:[52] Governor, salutes, suite and all; the Ionian explaining, etc. There is an interesting view of the plain of Kissamos, and the lower hills backed by the snow range, but it could not be tried on the ramparts, surrounded by a host of bores, on a narrow parapet. And so all at once (having been to see a small headless Apollo, and a column upside down) I thought I would go and sleep at Dhrapaniá, where 'Grace of God' [Theoháris, literally translated] Armenákis lives, as preferable to this horrid town, and also further on the morrow's road. No sooner planned than executed. Zeriff packed the things again, and I wished goodbye to the complimentious but good Cerigotto and came away at 4.40.

4.40 View of Kissamos. 5.15 Village; fine plain of olives and corn; view of Palaiókastro. 5.30 We ford the Typhlós: lovely olive and corn dells, and shades on soft hills. Olive groves and turtles.

I reached Dhrapaniá at six, having forded the Typhlós at 5.30. On the eighty-minutes walk many lovely bits were passed, but I dared not stop, nor were they more than usual, or very characteristic: undulating green cornfields and a perpetual spread of olives, with the Palaiókastro and the Topólia hills beyond, and near Kissamos the snow range also. Near Dhrapaniá, we fell into the same delightful shady lanes between endless olives by which we left this place two days back, and at the village, which is of considerable size (80 houses, but almost hidden; the low roofless habitations seldom peering above the trees), I was received most heartily by Theoháris and Michaélis Armenákis. A large and cleanish barny room — «τό ἰδικό σου» ['your very own'] — is given me, and we sit and talk on a house top of the same level. Armenákis thinks I *may* get to Haniá tomorrow, but I hardly think this possible. We talk till past eight. 'God's Grace' runs up and down actively, with a few apologies for delay now and then, and after a while supper comes; and what it had been had they expected me I do not know. Two stewed turtles and excellent pilaf, eggs also, which I sent away as 'troppo' [too much], very decent wine, though not like that of Ghoniá or Topólia. But with these Cretans, the most remarkable thing is their manly heartiness and eagerness to please, unencumbered by compliments. 'You must forgive all drawbacks — my house is out of order — his brother is to be married tomorrow — and his wife expects her confinement every hour — and you know you came at sunset, and unexpected, or you should not have had so much to complain of.' This man is more plain and hearty and English than most Southerners generally. It is now 9.30. I am writing in bed, and have made this small Cretan house vastly comfortable. George and Zeriff are supping below. 9.40 Both return and go to their particular beds. Owls do cry; one is close to my window. I always like that bird's voice.

Slept tolerably well, but the church bells bothered at 2 or 3 a.m. George slept on his bed at t'other end of the large lofty room, Zeriff on a divan. At 5.30 we are all ready, but the host and his family are at church, as are all the villagers. The *papás* [priest] is praying endless over a vast bunch of flowers and lighted tapers, and everybody is lighting little tapers thereat.[53] 6 We are loading, and Theoháris has brought a lot of eggs (pleasant people and good). Off at six.

7 First fountain. 8.10–15 Second, or Spiliá fountain. 8.40 Cross little stream and make away from Ghoniá hills. At eleven we pass the Plat600 on a mule, as it is too deep for walking, and at 11.15 reach a *khan* below the town — oy! vot a valk!

Notes: The first hour we went *round* Ta Nopíghia, and passed a bridge; lovely

SATURDAY
30 APRIL

DHRAPANIA
SPILIA
PLATANIA
HALEPA

49

Flowing like a crystal river
(The Poet's Mind.)

Platanià.
Crete.

morning quiet, ἀηδόνια [nightingales], etc. The second hour was a hard pull upwards, but light work down, the morning hill air being very pleasant. 8.10 We were at the fountain. From 8.15 to 9.15 we crossed the last Ghoniá hills (Cape Spadha), and went on over the half-desert ground above the sea, making straight for Platanià. Crossed several oleander streams and so, nearing the sea line ever, reached the river at eleven. George and I commence to cross it, but find it too deep [[at least for me who cannot swim]] — above hips in one part — so we retreat and hire a moke for 2d and pass over, stopping at the second *khan* close below the town at 11.15. Here we lunch on bread, one egg (I weary of eggs), good wine and a new institution — herrings. Verily this walk is, as Zeriff says, «ἀληθῶς τρομερά» ['truly frightful']. Peasant man comes and sits and talks; asks me to go to his province — Selino [Palaiohóra] — and offers brother to travel in England. Start off 12.45; at city gate 3.15; Halépa 3.45 — just three hours. George horrid cross; I much more so: 'the fault was mine'.[54] These long heating walks irritate such tempers but I ought to be more tranquil and less touchy, which I ain't. George complains of the Topólia accommodation, which pickups I ought to have spoken of, and I growl equally at monastery arrangements — neither of the laments being wholly just. At the Consulate the kind Hays received me delightfully, ditto Madeleine. A thorough tub and wash set me up: and later a dinner divine of pilaf and mutton and fried potatoes and salad and good wine. Sat talking with the Hays till 8.45, then bed.

Very clear and lovely, but windy. Slept soundly till two or three, when the Easter uproar began and ceased not: knocking at doors and letting off pistols and crackers without limit. «Χριστός ἀνέστη» ['Christ is risen']: and very uncomfortable it is that people believe he did so. George came up at six, as good as ever, and I told him I am sorry I had spoken so angrily [[but he said, grinning, 'Sarebbe stupida la vita senza qualche rabbia alle volte' ['Life would be stupid without some flare-ups at times']]]. Verily he is a brick. Took some magnesia and coffee, and wrote journal and placed drawings till nine or ten, when I walked in the gallery with the Hays. From twelve, slept and read, and at one, dinner. (Guarracino called earlier.) Extremely pleasant. The Anglo-Oriental picturesque cleanliness of this house is delightful; the friendliness of Hay and Mrs Hay, her beauty and the engaging child, all are pleasures. At four: they are all gone out walking, 'but I desire to rest'.[55] George plays with the monkey. He says the city is full of patrols; and doubtless this letting off firearms is a fearful bore. When they returned Mr and Mrs Hay and I play with the ape and walk till seven; then tea, and later sang and played, and bed at nine.

SUNDAY
1 MAY

HALEPA

Absolutely! all things are gray and it rains! not much though. Firing pistols still goes on. Finished reading *Villette* — a very lovely book.[56] Rose, arranged paper and clothes for three or four weeks, and wrote out journal till eleven, also finishing Mrs Clive's letter and one to Signor Moazza. The kindness of these Hays is incomparable: they never bother me any way and are always doing me good. He told me yesterday that none of his family know of his marriage. Before dinner and after I sang a good deal to them, and then read quietly, till at five we three walked out to a dell of olives and sat (I drawing the distant Haniá for a time) till we walked slowly back by another route. Their love of flowers and scenery and nature altogether is most pleasant. The two dogs run up walls and over houses. Little Madeleine comes and meets us as we return and then follow music, walking the gallery, tea, and then music till bed-time — nine. I hear (it is nine now) little Madeleine crying and think she is not well. I have seldom passed a pleasanter day than this for a long time.

MONDAY
2 MAY

HALEPA

Breakfast at eight with the Hays. Newspapers. 9.30 Set off down to Bay of Suda. Fine view of bay. 10.15 Low marshy plain — Tuzla: saltworks, a few cafés, warehouses, etc. 10.30 Bay of Suda; good wide road. Flat long lines of Akrotíri. Eleven: narrow bay, black arums — smell. 11.15 Ascend. Plane and rill. 11.30 Ascent — and leave road to Kalýves on left; second fountain and fig tree. 11.45 Great ascent: top, 11.50. Turn left:

TUESDAY
3 MAY

HALEPA
SUDA BAY

scattery village cum pigs; Apokórona below, and Sphakiá mountains — cloudy. 12.30 Near *metóhi* [dependency of a monastery], having lost our way and returned. Monastery: courtyard, many men and women and pigs and children; priest's room, *rakí*,[57] etc. *Hegoúmenos* — dull man. Lunch at two. Cloudier. Take man as guide to walls. Nothing can be more mortifying after such trouble and expense than to find all thrown away; through cloud everywhere. Ida, Sphakiá, all invisible; not even Akrotíri nor Cape Dhrepanon discernible! Walls magnificent, but could do next to nothing for it began to rain. Walked round walls. Write this at four, having come in from the rain. Beastly noisy boy. Fooly *kalógheros* [monk], blessing God for the English affection and benefits towards Greece. Zeriff says nothing. Red waistcoats of men, laced behind. Guide said, pointing to the walls and entrance of Aptera, «Ἐδῶ ἤτανε τὸ γκέττο, διὰ τοὺς Ἑβραίους» ['here was the ghetto, for the Jews']: a nook in the walls. At four it began to rain as we were near some finer, but less old, bits of wall, and then I came in to the *kalógheros's* room, when it rained hard. The *kalógheros* asks many questions about me and George. Zeriff says we can sleep at the Monastery of Karídhi tomorrow, at Episkopí on Thursday and Rethymnon on Friday.

When we set out to see the walls a quiet peasant accompanied me, and showed all very well. Some are very grand and fine, like Tiryns; others like Krani, though not nearly so good. Yet the views of Akrotíri and of Dhrepanon would have been quite splendid had it been fine, and the Sphakiá view glorious if any hills could be at all seen. To make the vexation worse, a beastly little boy made a continual row, till I sent him back, being irritated beyond all bounds. All was mist and rain.

From 4.30 to seven have gone as best it might in the *kalógheros's* room. Lord! how dirty it is! The rain, however, not ceasing and the wind increasing. Converse little. The *kalógheros* is dull; a very weary man of Patmos, to the monastery of which the land here belongs — St John the Theologian. He spoke of the Διάδοχος [the Prince of Wales] and General Bruce [[with A. P. Stanley, whom he called «ὁ διδάσκαλος κι' ὁ ἱερεύς του» ['his teacher and priest']]], having been at Patmos when they came.[58] «Ὤ τί μεγάλη δυστυχία!» ['What a great misfortune!'] he continued to howl when I said General Bruce was dead. [[Even Zeriff, who listens to all but says nothing, was half alarmed: and after a time, particularly when he began to talk of Turkey and of England's protection of Greece, I was obliged to tell him that the Sultan was a friend of my Queen, as well as the King of Greece.]] He acts as steward here for five years. At seven food was brought: *dolmás* (rice and meat in vine leaves), and we had our own cold lamb and *baccalà* [dried salted fish], bread and cheese and a little wine — here there is none. The objectionable boy stood and stared, and the old women also. A most filthy napkin nearly made me sick, so unclean are these people. Good coffee after, and at 8.45 we cleared the room. Then good George made my bed on one side, and now I am in it. Zeriff on the farther sofa, and George on the one nearer. George's quiet attendance is a very great blessing, but I really doubt if I can go through much more of this Cretan life. There are no signs of better weather tomorrow, and I can't decide what to do: go back, go on or wait. Meanwhile, vermin and *dreadful* sufferings.

Neohóri, 4 May.

WEDNESDAY
4 MAY

APTERA
ARMENI
KARYDHI
EXOPOLIS

Dreadful sufferings. *No* sleep at all: vermin, blasts of wind, and snoring. So terrible a night it is long since I have passed, and it is only 1.30 a.m. now! A knowledge of Cretan Topography would be hardly gained thus, even if one could make drawings; but with such torture added to the entire throwing-away of time and money! Bah!

5.30 It is fine, thank God! We are packed, and George and I are going out. 7.45 I am back at the very nasty room, St John of Patmos staring, and Mrs St John fanning the coffee. I and George have been able to go all round the walls, and I to draw Ida and what-not; the Sphakian mountains being delightfully clear. Everywhere from the circuit of this ancient place there is a fine view, but the vast hollow of Apokórona plain, backed by the snowy range and seen between crags of a pale gray or nearly white, is magnificent. With the Roman remains I could do nothing; but the end of Akrotíri with Dhrepanon are fine. Well: so far one has to be thankful.

Off, 8.30, I giving the silly *kalógheros* 20 piastres, who came some way with us. At nine, going down an odious stony descent and making for the plain; the landscape vast and imposing, though wanting in character as to detail. We are to go and halt at Arméni, and to sleep at Karýdhi. 9.15 Below Aptera. Magnificent green valley, and clear line of snow mountains. 9.30 I and George pass the river, on foot. It was *awfully* cold, and rapid, and up above my knees, and I funked cramp. We had to cross direct, and then zigzag, to avoid holes and currents, but Zeriff knew all well. The scene was

53

green and delightful; dark green foliage and snow beyond. After which we went along green fertile fields, here and there by muddy paths or lanes, here and there by viler pavements, till we reached Arméni: an Ottoman village chiefly — mosque outside, and with wooden bazaars and water channels reminding me of Macedonia. At 10.30 we unload at a 'General Shop' and eat: cold lamb, *baccalà* — the shop like most in Akrídha and elsewhere. It is odd enough to hear Mussulmen and Christians all speaking Greek. Blues predominate in dress, but there are red broad belts and caps and waistcoats — or the latter are black. Nasty wine, but a polite Greek in sober dress brought me some good [[but not even this act determined the religion of the donor, as it would in other Moslem places, for here the Mussulmen as well as the Christian Greeks all drink wine]]. Men and women all very large and fine. Boughs on a rough wooden trellis make a shade, and swallows flit thereunder. Gleams in cool greens a plane tree: beyond I see the Sphakian snow. *Nargilehs* are the mode. The river we crossed was the Sphakorýako; Kiliáris [is the name of] river next Kalýves, which names a Greek tells me, and an *Othomanós*, who take me to see great springs of water and planes in a nearby garden. Returning, at 11.30, we prepare to go. No-one will take any money for anything — ! — and another Greek, Manouélis Ierakákis, gives me an ornamented Easter-circular-egg-bedecked bread; the wine-giver was Iannákis Papalá-kis. Arméni is called in Turkish Tistiklí. Off at twelve, up stony hill. Snake — dead — at 12.15. Akrotíri seems all one with the land; the Aptera a flat and level height, and all the rest becomes very ugly.

A hideous stony undulating ascent succeeds, shutting out all, and at 12.45 we are at the top: anything uglier one cannot imagine. 1 We come to a wide stony Cerigo-like tract — long ugly lines: Vamos and all the end of Dhrepanon visible, but with no hope of beauty. Vamos, 1.30: stop for water. 2 After *horrid* roads, we come in sight of Karýdhi: a broad low valley below great hills and the snow range. Arrive at two; apparently at a village, but really a cluster of *metóhia*. Surprising to relate, a sturdy blue-clad *kalógheros* said, «Μέ δυσκολία ἔχεις νὰ κοιμηθῆς ἐδῶ» ['it'll be difficult for you to sleep here']; and an older fellow said «Δὲν ἔχομε καθαρὸ σπίτι» ['we haven't got a clean house']; 'the *Hegoúmenos* was away', etc. etc. In fact they would not take us in, and Zeriff oddly did not seem to like to press them. We got a glass of superexcellent wine, and prepare to go in disgust. Descend, and rise again, by very pleasing olive parky ground. 3 p.m. always broad olives and corn, and long mountain lines, but *nothing* novel. Horrid, but very picturesque, roads and some fine deep dells. At 3.45 arrive at [Exópolis] and wait at a filthy pothouse outside the ruinous village, while the *Proestós* [village president] is sent to. If I am to suffer again tonight I shall make straight for Rethymnon tomorrow and travel here no more. Torture, and nothing gained by it, is a bore. [Exópolis] is a most miserable place; no decent house can be found, and we must abide in this pothouse. No wine either. Meanwhile, things grow more odious in that pothouse: several drunken Greeks were there, and some sober but angry Turx [[both parties being armed it seems likely some row will ensue, and it does not require much travelling in Crete to perceive that its elements are extremely

Lake Kourná, 9 a.m., 5 May.

volcanic]]. In vain we tried two houses or rooms: more filthy still, and the *Proestós* was out. And it was too late to return to Karýdhi and too far to go to Episkopí. [[The journey from Haniá to Rethymnon is either performed by steamer or in a single day by horsemen, so that there are no places of any kind used as dwellings by travellers between the two towns.]] So I made up my mind to stay with the disgusting drunkards and beggars and filthy people.

Later however the *Proestós*, Harálambi, came and we got an upper empty room, where at seven I write this. At 7.45 asparagus salad, lamb and *baccalà* and good wine. Three Cretans sit and stare. The little owl doth cry; the fleas do bite. Also the Cretans stare at my going to bed. George and Zeriff sleep in the same room.

How the darling owls did cry! But, thank God, I slept very well. Rose at four, and at 5.30 (having paid 10 piastres to host) left this piggery, and came out with George to the church above, where I drew till 6.30, a pleasant and fine expanse. During all yesterday, this, and the view from above Karýdhi, are the only two I could have wished to draw, and the latter was not clear as to distance and so useless, as it was mainly a rich olive-covered valley scene. Certainly, Crete has few very picturable

55

scenes hitherto, though it is full of loveliness. I go now to the filthy café of last afternoon, and mean to go and see Kourná. The abundant richness and greenness of the scene before me, and the quiet, are charms not often got nowadays: what fields! what a land of food and riches! O land! O Crete! O morning!

Café, and off at 6.30. Stony descent. Most lovely morning! Fresh green-lanes, as it were. Low olives. And I and George wait to listen to the ἀηδόνια [nightingales] who are wonderful. 7.15 Draw river scene, which at seven I and George forded barefoot — great fun. Freshness and nightingales. 7.30 Ruins of Armyró and fountain with two planes. Great stream. Mills. Plain. 7.45 Leave Rethymnon road and go up hill slightly towards Kourná. Ground very lovely — parky green — large clumps of great oak: δρύϊα, [dhrýia] not βελανίδα [velanídha].[59] Zeriff says there were great numbers of these trees, but they have been cut down; indeed we saw two being burned to make them fall. This spot is quite delightful, cistus and myrtle everywhere.

8.30 We are at the Lake of Kourná — very fine and Cumberlandish — in a nook at the foot of very high hills. Draw, and at nine come to trees not far off, leaving the very beastly-forlorn metóhi sort of house close to the lake. «Ἐκοιμηθήκαμε μαζί μὲ τὰ γουρούνια μιὰ φορά εἴς τὶς εἴκοσι τέσσερις ὥρας· καὶ δὲν φθάνει;» ['We've slept with pigs once in twenty-four hours; isn't that enough?'], says George, [who] is gone a-wild grapes getting. (George says, while I was drawing this morning, a man kept taking lice out of his head and killing them with the edge of the coffee pot.) We have sent the chap of the metóhi, who has brought us a jug, for a cuccuma [coffee pot] — «ἀλλὰ δὲν εὑρίσκεται» ['but there isn't one to be found'] — also for some glasses, my tin cup being broken. All this morning's walk has been most enjoyable, and the nearer one gets to Ida the more chance there seems of the lines becoming finer, for hitherto they are meagre. At ten we breakfast or lunch: the lamb and baccalà are finished, a thousand birds sing, shade of trees delightful; and this pleasure even seems to make amends for past bother and torture. The four sitting Cretans are wholly tranquil in manner, and discourse a few now and then quietly. I wish I had made a drawing of Ida between the large oaks. 11.15 Lunch is done: the wrens and titmice still sing — still. Zeriff hubblebubbles. The four Cretan creturs sleep, and the sun comes over the oak tree I lie beneath so I must move. Very delightful hours, like those — somewhat — of the days that are no more. I hear from George that the real Hegoúmenos of the Karýdhi Monastery is in prison, on suspicion of having aided his brother in the death of a man killed in the monastery. I thought something was wrong: but why did Zeriff take us there? The three Cretans opened on this when I praised the monastery wine, and Zeriff quietly said, 'He has been in φυλακή [prison] for three months already, and τόσο [much] is offered for the head of the murderer.'

Noon. We prepare to go: lovely air! and most beautiful mountain spot! What blackbirds! 12–12.30 We wind up a myrtle-grown hillside, making towards the sea; this lake evidently lies 'unwholesomely' low, but the mountains about it are fine. Yet, looking back towards Exópolis and Dhrepanon, the scene is very uninteresting and formless. 1 p.m. Always going up a more and more bare hillside: stunty myrtles and

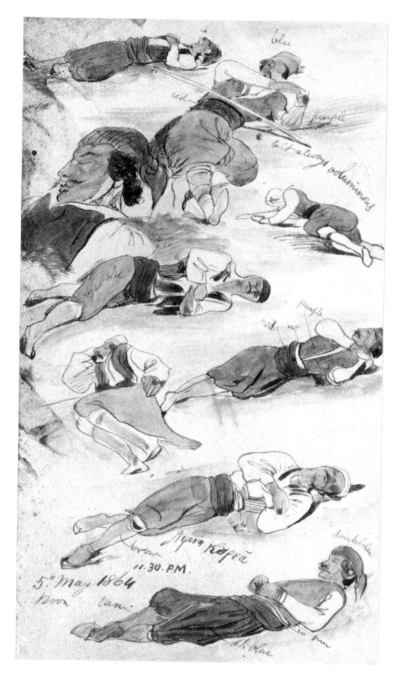

Lake Kourná, 11.30 p.m. [a.m.!], 5 May.

cistus — few — and one or two oleander rivulets. At top: nearing Dhramia, which looks a ruin, and behind is the plain I drew this morning from Exópolis; in the middle the long formless promontery of Dhrepanon — right — and the upper part of the Kourná hills — left — with the snow Sphakian range beyond all. At 1.10 pass

Dhramia, and see Episkopí beyond. Dhramia is apparently all in ruins, though with signs of former size. 1.30 Ford small river. 2 Ever going uphill, nearing Episkopí, which *looks*, but I dare say *is not*, better than the last hole. A fine open hilly country; olive plantations about, and corn.

Episkopí proved to be, like the last, more than half in ruins, and the streets or lanes more filthy, as being fuller of inhabitants, the place being larger, and Turks many. Along very insupportable places, we reach the Doctor's house, which Zeriff proposes to go to, I having no letter: but he is out. A relation however came, fat and in a swell Levantine dress, and he orders things indoors: a large, decent, stone-paved room; divan at one end, three windows on one side, portraits of King and Queen opposite, books and vials at t'other end. All the women sent off; coffee and water and thenceforth, talk. Doctor, master of the house and brother-in-law of fat man, and very deaf, came in. We all went out to see a view, passing very nasty bazaar and then downhill. After that we came back and sat again, and then I washed in public.

Later, in pure despair, we went to a garden and examined beans and other vegetables, and now — 6.15 — I sit in hopes of change. Supper at 7.15: a rough sort of cove the brother-in-law, but the Doctor, poor fellow, has much of the gentleman in him. Odd mixture of things! He says 'pardon' in French, and talks about Mazzini and Garibaldi. Rice soup, boiled lamb, eggs and stew — roast with capital Kissamos wine and nuts. Fat cove made his little daughter eat extreme before she went to bed, and then talked to me about the Doctor, who supports his mother and grandmother: «Ἡ γιαγιά του· αὐτή εἶναι ἴσως σχεδόν ἐνενήντα χρονῶν.» ['His grandmother; she's perhaps almost ninety years old.'] Fat man wanted George and Zeriff to sit down when we did: «Εἶναι κι' ἄνθρωποι ἐλεύθεροι» ['they are free men too'], but George and Zeriff didn't. Talked as much as I could, and had the bed made in sight of the family, ὥς διδασκαλία [as a lesson]. At nine got the room clear; 9.30, bed.

**FRIDAY
6 MAY**

**EPISKOPI
RETHYMNON**

Slept well; few fleas, and the two men were quiet. Rose 4.30. The Doctor is Odhyssévs Stravroianídhis, and the fat friend Vasílios Dhrandhákis. Coffee and leave-taking. Off 5.45. Horrid lanes of stones, impeded by sheep, etc. etc. etc. State of ruined villages. 6.15 Open out on cultivated hills with sea beyond and the two capes. Day cloudy. 6.30 Descend nearer the sea: the view here would be magnificent were not all the mountains quite invisible. 6.45 Seashore. 7 Arrive at the Petrés Kamára river, coming through a grand dark gorge and broken bridge. Cross on ass.

7.45 We have been going up and coming down the Kakó Vounó [Bad Mountain], by most execrable stone staircase roads. The coast east is full of long point-promonteries with a foreground of black and gray any-part-of-English-coast rocks. West, the long strip of Dhrepanon and the Akrotíri hills — hidden. All much trouble and little gain. 8.15 Same bother. A more horrid coast edge of sharp rocks can't be! 8.40 Leave sea, but ever on grim dry rox, over vast undulations. 8.45 Ravine, opening on sea, dreadful hard rocky path: half way.

10 Rethymnon seen afar. 10.15 Ever this horrible Murgie [in Apulia] endless

Rethymnon coast, Bay of Armyró, 9.30 a.m., 6 May.

stone path! We have met an Arab girl, then an enquiring black, then anxious elderly female. 10.30 Send on Zeriff to Rethymnon, and stop to suck a lemon and draw. Got down to the sea at 11.10, where there is some water, which aids us to eat some bread and O! cheese! in a shady kiosk, overflowing with goats. We return to rocks above the sea, where I draw till 12.30. Town relieves from sea in dark bits and bright sparkles here and there. At the town, passing by leper village, and at Mr George Kalokairi-nós's[60] house by 1.30. Complimentary and fussy old cove.

I have come to a *(very)* inner room, to write a bit after a lunch of beefsteaks, olives, eggs and good wine. The long road brought us towards Rethymnon: the fortress is a large but not very picturesque affair, but the wide cemeteries seem to speak of more Mussulman life here than hitherto. At 1.20 Zeriff met us on the walls, with a fat, similarly-habited man, some retainer of the Kalokairinós' and him we followed by diabolical pavements through a dark arch and very bothery empty dirty bazaars to the Vice-Consular house. Immediately Kyrios George Kalokairinós met me, an elderly and rather vinous grcat Ccrigotto, but far too fussy — removing my hat, sack, etc. — more than was bearable. However, he seemed willing to be good natured, only rather drunky. Small child and fat man (son-in-law) and George and Zeriff sat by. After much fuss, which I ignored in quiet (the room was pleasant and large), I was taken to lunch, and that meal was very satisfactory so far as food went. But the old gent wants me to visit the Governor and the Bey, and I *won't*. There is an elderly wife, small and bird-like, and a rather handsome daughter, wife of the fat man, and many others. Mr Kalokairinós proposes to walk with me this evening, and to go to some villages tomorrow — where, I don't know. In so short a stay of two or three days in such places it is a toss-up if one gains or loses more by not giving in to a cumbrous destiny of this kind, let it be that the civility of such houses demand some self-denial. Meanwhile I am here, but George is gone out with Zeriff and this small room is literally a heap of φορτώματα [baggage]. (None of the people here seem to have the least idea of distances towards Kastro [Herákleion] or Gortyn. Foolishness abounds.) When George came back I got a thorough wash and went out to the sitting room, when George did likewise. Came a son of Mr Kalokairinós — Levantine — civil. Coffee, and at five the old gent came with two boys and his son-in-law and we all 'went out for a walk'. Very little sufficed to show me that there is little to do at Rethymnon: but we went up a gully and above to a saint's tomb and old Kalokairinós nearly bored me to death; returning by another gate and street and declining to see the port. At the house, found they had six men putting up a bed! — and all the children and women besides — so the room is useless for the present. Was wroth and irritated, but sat with the old cove who is a *frightful* bore, and talks of the 'Governo' *ad nauseam*. Supper proclaimed. Two Anatolic sea-captains, and a gawky son at school at Syra: two captains seemed to me far better bred than all the rest, who clawed food out of the dishes, etc. etc. It cost me an effort to break up the party at nine, when lo! I found George had made up my own little bed! He says the other 'fell all to pieces'. 9.30 Am in bed, but people rush in and out, and altogether Rethymnon is a bore.

<table>
<tr><td>

SATURDAY
7 MAY

RETHYMNON
PERIVOLIA
RETHYMNON

</td><td>

Horrid hot box of a room! Yet I slept tolerably. Bugs alas! Rose at five, dressed, left bed, etc., gave a note to Zeriff, who I regret leaves me here, and paid him for his seven days' horse hire. And at six, came out with George and drew on the east side of the town and in various places till nine. Again, above (and through the village of Perivólia), near Aghios Gheórghios till 10.30. 'What are those birds?' says I to a peasant: «Εἴναι μελισσοφάγοι.» ['They are bee-eaters.'] (Owls also last night.) At 10.30 we suddenly resolved to go to the sands, [it] being as George says, «Εὐχαρίστησις κοντά στὴν θάλασσα» ['a pleasure near the sea'], so down we came; a most clear and lovely sea, with only the long snow-fretted lines of mountains not blue. So we made a lunch of very surprising cold soles and *triglia* [barbels], eggs, bread and cheese

</td></tr>
</table>

Perivólia, 2 p.m., 7 May. (Lear has mistakenly put the date of 8 May on this drawing.)

Rethymnon, 6.30 p.m., 7 May.

and *stupendous* wine, and very pleasant it was till 11.30, when it grew hot and we mizzle at 11.45. We go back to the Perivólia villages where all were occupied *shadoofing* and sit us down below a mulberry tree — a very pleasant hour — to 1 p.m.

2 p.m. Still wandering about the 'gardens' [*perivólia*, literally translated] or sitting in the shade of the mulberry tree. Two wonderful things exist in Crete — facts: 1. no dogs bark or bite, except at other dogs; 2. nobody bothers you. Few or none of these peasants can ever have seen two Europeans so clad and acting, yet they only say, 'Is the shade pleasant?' and then «καλό» ['good'], walking away with no further sign. How are we to get through tomorrow? and most of Monday? However, nearly half our mournful task is done already. These garden folk seem to live a pleasant life, and sing to their *shadoofs*: vegetable marrows and various vegetables appear to thrive well.

It is now four, and we have come to the end of the walls, and as George is athirst I have sent him in for water. Certainly, a most meagre place is Rethymnon, and what to do tomorrow I know not. Anatolian sheep. Went up the hill partly we ascended last night, and drew till six: and now I have exhausted all the feeble resources of this place, the which is a bore. We returned slowly and by the filthy lanes; got home by 6.30.

61

Rethymnon, 6.30 a.m., 9 May.

Wash and dawdle till seven; at 7.30 supper and suffering. Draw a whale over my torchers. The converse was mostly on soap.[61] O dirt! Bed at 9.30.

Rose at five. In council with George it was fixed as 'too brutto' to leave the family all today; so we arrange to come back before noon. Coffee at 6.15, and at 6.30 we wander on the ramparts, the world being clear and blue. Then we come down to the sea, which is perfectly calm and like a large opal mirror, and we sit on the sand and asphodels till 9.30, I writing to Spiro and T. Cooper, and my journal up to April 30; but it grows hot, and we must prepare to face an afternoon at Rethymnon. Meanwhile, as I walk about, little boy brings me large bunch of lettuces (μαρούλια). I thought he was taking them somewhere else, but he came up and said, «Πάρε τοῦτα» ['take these'], and when I only said I would take one: «Πάρε ὅλα» ['take them all']. So I took them and George has gone to wash them in the sea. (A small sort of aloe with yellow flowers grows here plentifully.) Little boy ran away quickly, and was no more found.

10.30 We dawdled back, heat already beginning to be great. The long lines of Rethymnon are a bore, but the clear sparkle of the city and the broad band of Sphakian snow white separating lilac and blue is fine, in the mountain distance.[62] Back by 11.15 and I retired to arrange paper and wash. At twelve, food — O lord! what a piggy feed! — the matter tolerable, the manner loathsome. At 1.30 we have come out, and I sit writing, or read Pashley till four, or slept. Afterwards, coffee; the children all get to George, who is kind to everybody always. Went with Mr Kalokairinós to see his son: pleasing wife, nice baby, roomy new house. Sit in gallery and sketch Ida, which in colour is lovely. Returned at 6.30, the elder Kalokairinós bemoaning life in Rethymnon as 'barbaro', among 'barbari' — as, poor man, well he may. His smaller son takes a fancy to George and won't leave him. The elder Kalokairinós says he knows many cases of leprosy coming on at 30 or 40 years of age, without parental descent, and believes it to be caused by overmuch oil and salt diet. Ἀλάδανο [Aládhano] or dittany, a perfumed herb, is gathered about Melidhóni and sold; much valued by the Turks.[63]

Rethymnon, 8 a.m., 9 May.

After half an hour's talk with Mr Kalokairinós and the two Anatolical captains (who are waiting for their ships to have a cargo of oil), also with the handsome and amiable married daughter, whose husband Harálambos is piggy and good-natured, we went to supper. Boiled lamb, some Turkish dish, and a vast heap of *μυζηθρόπηττες* [cheese pies] (and to see Mr Harálambos eat these — twelve — one at a single mouthful! and last night to see him similarly eat raw beans!), with two sorts of wine, both *good thoroughly*. There came in also a big Sphakiot man, like John Gould[64] and Thackeray piled together; and also another whose face expressed more cunning and silliness than could be portrayed. So we talked and smoked, but very little was drunk, till 9.30 — then bed. George has, as usual, made my bed and bedroom perfectly comfortable, and considering the bore, 'pare un'anno oggi', has been totally patient and good; all the children going to him in swarms by instinct. So much for my fourth week in Crete.

At the end of one of the streets here, is a round bright blue bit of wood with 'Zitzo' written on it in gold letters. We thought it a name of an inn, or a man. But it is the quarter of the town.

Rose at four, and got all things packed. Coffee by five, and off 5.15, sitting on the ramparts drawing till seven. The lepers at both gates are horrible here. We also went on the sands till nearly nine, and then to the port, to Austrian Lloyd's about the steamer, returning 'home' by 10.15. Pretty hot it is. T'other captain's ship has arrived.

('In Corfu there are always little one-eyed men on whom you can walk below the olive trees': my mistake, *μονομάτια* [one-eyed] for *μονοπάτια* [foot-paths], in describing Corfu.) It is not every day one has a present of lettuces; let us be thankful therefore.

What a pavement is this of Rethymnon! I buy a good blanket of Sphakian make for 300 piastres.

At twelve we dine: George Kalokairinós, Mr Harálambos and the pleasant woman his wife. After dinner talked with Kalokairinós, disturbed by small children's outbreax, about the island, etc. He is after all a kindly cove, but the sneaky Ionian manner is a bore. Abruptiously the steamer is announced. More abruptly a second summons, and we rush out, I beholding three large black men taking all my *roba*. The children jump and shriek 'all over the place', George endeavours to penetrate the *harem* or γυναικών to thank Mrs Harálambos, but only meets the old lady and not the Graziosa. The old lady (who is the most frightful caricature of Lady Farquhar possible)[65] twirls about and says, «Τὶ νὰ κάμουμε;» ['What are we to do?'] Rethymnon life draws to a clothes. Altogether the proximate advent of the *atmópleon* [steamer] is an interesting circumstance. George, who never forgets those who are kind to him, is bebothered at not being able to thank Mrs H. It is only 1.30 now; steamer not in. Endless fuss. I go to the 'shop' or *empórion;* George looks after the luggage. Fuss at *Dogana* — very ridiculous. At last, off in a boat about 2.30. Found Consul Hay on board (and Henry Moazza), but he is not going ashore, for they say we are to start soon.

And so we did, at 2.45 or 3, to my surprise. Very fine and smooth. Rethymnon soon faded away, and no particular beauty followed.

Dinner. The jokes of the three captains of the *Persia* are not appreciated. After dinner on deck; some views of Ida are fine, but it is soon lost behind the great northern bluff coast cliffs. Near Candia [Herákleion] the scene opens out at once, and is at least promising so far as being wide and open, with Mount Juktas very conspicuous. Great delay and immense row in landing, the port being very small. Bore in the boat, and in going ashore: a hustle and savagery not outdone in Jaffa. The landing was a regular misery. We go to the Vice-Consul's house (he having come off for Mr Hay) and preceded by many lanterns thread the dark streets for a short distance and arrive at Mr Kalokairinós',[66] where several courts, etc., lead to a large room: the Consul has a bedroom out of this; I one full of boxes and very nasty, up a narrow stair; a clerk, Moazza and G. Kalokairinós sleeping in closets out of this again. Supper is served. Mrs Kalokairinós speaks a little French and is a nice sort of woman. The Vice-Consul is a pleasant little man, and very rich. Hay not eating, and they pressing him, are mutual bores. Bed at eleven. A most horrible and filthy amount of bugs developed, on my bed and all over the place.

<table>
<tr><td>TUESDAY
10 MAY

HERAKLEION</td><td>O bugs! I caught 34! Read newspapers. Rose 5.50. Poor George has got no sleep as the hole he is put into is filthier than where I am. Out on the walls at 6.30 with a fat guide. Ruined cathedral, ruined but splendid walls and fortifications. Views of Mount Juktas, and of Ida. Town mealy-ruiny, earthquaky, odious. We return at nine from going round the walls, from which are good views of Juktas and Ida, but the aspect of the distance is rather large than lovely. The Consul has to hear no end of affairs from Kalokairinós, and I found it no easy matter to wedge in questions relating to my own plans. I intend to go round Ida as far as may be coincident with a possible future plan</td></tr>
</table>

Kapetánios Michael Korakas
(from a photograph by
Cl. Androulakis).

of going into Sphakiá by the south coast. Henry Moazza helps me with names, and I am introduced to one Kapetánios Michael Korakas,[67] who is to meet me at Ambeloúzo and to further instruct me. At Askýphou, if I ever get there, I am to ask for one Ioánnis Vandhínos. (The Korakas is called the Garibaldi of Crete, and is now in the Turkish Government's pay — only they don't pay him.) At Dhaphnés I am to go to one [Manuél] Bernardhákis.

The walk round the walls this morning: utter ruin and mishmash *qua* town and forts, but much picturesqueness *qua* distance; Juktas and Ida, which last however seems only a higher snow range of a long and rather gloomy wall of hills. Below it, looking east, the plains are green; but it is hardly possible to make any drawing of any part of the city, which lies low sloping to the sea, and is of uniformly flat-topped houses, broken mosques and palms here and there. The Venetian cathedral, a ruin-skeleton, speaks of former days. We came back by the bazaars — very ordinary and disagreeable — only the streets are somewhat wider than in other towns. Altogether a nastier and less interesting Turkish town I was never in, and the paved streets are frightful. At ten, having returned, I slept, and Mrs Kalokairinós came and apologized for the B flats.[68]

Knossos, 8 a.m., 11 May.

Hay and Moazza went off at 3 a.m. to shoot rabbits at Dhia. Up and dressed by 5.15: only killed 16 bugs — 16 only. This city is like a large dish, the ramparts being the raised edge and all the rest being one monotonous mass of houses, nearly all flat and low, and a great part of the space being full of the ruins caused by the earthquake of 11th October 1856. A good number of palms give the place a more oriental look than that of any other in Crete, but the interior of the city is of the same mongrel European character as to its bazaars: ropes and cotton handkerchiefs being the chief objects for sale. Off from the mishmash of ten dirty women at 5.45, with a slow man. We pass a Turkish cemetery for a long way, having gone out of the ponderous walls by the Kainoúria Gate. Juktas fine. Pass a *tavérna*, with picturesque olives and 'mouvement de terre', and leaving the road to Fortétsa to the right, go by lanes between cornfields, and are soon near Makrý Teihos, near the foot of the hills, where there is a stream and trees below. The site of Knossos possesses water and trees and plenty of *aïdhónia*, [nightingales], but except scattered masses of brickwork, little remains. The place however with its green hillside slopes and corn has a pretty aspic. Go on to the valley, which is pretty and brimful of trees and nightingales. Draw till eight; George gathers watercresses. Walnuts, planes, olives, etc. Leave stream and go to the hill nearer Fortétsa: large stones, apparently of temple. It was near nine before we saw the lumpy shell of a tomb, called 'of Caiaphas', and past nine when we got up to Fortétsa where there are lots of middle-aged walls — or Byzantine — and many old stones (the village was half deserted) and I don't doubt it was the acropolis of Knossos once on a time.

9.10 Descend. The view is dry and Chieti-like yet full of culture — and not drawable. Candia is feeble and contemptible: whity ochre and green pervade the plain, which is much broken and conceals in hollows spots of olives and wide expanses of corn. Altogether the scene is unsatisfactory *qua* painting. The slow and wooden man

66

Megalókastro (Herákleion), 4 p.m., 10 May and 7 a.m., 12 May.

sent to guide us took us the way I didn't want to go, as we had to retrieve through cornfields and ploughed ground. 9.45 We reached a sort of 'metósshi',[69] as they pronounce it, and as there was an aqueduct of clear water, and some olives, we sat down to lunch. The Kalokairinós had given us some wine, bread and cheese in the morning, and had sent after us a second lot — meat and oranges — as we were on the way; so we did very well. At 10.30 I gave the slow man 10 piastres and sent him home. The day was warm, but with light clouds hiding the sun and giving us shadows. But Ida is clear, though ugly, for its base is all cut up by sad lines. The ripple of the water, through a hole in the aqueduct, is ever pleasant. I sit and write. George pokes about hedges and fields. Black man comes, and little boy, and peasants, and I draw them. They are all good tempered and laugh; small boy almost cries at drawing of a donkey, and is impelled to give me two lemons. I gave him a pencil. Peasants like Life Guardsmen. 1 p.m.

At 1.30 we 'wander on', and at two, near a sort of tavern previously passed, I draw till 2.30 by the side of a ravine, which ought to be made picturesque in a drawing, with the olives etc. about and the snowy Lasíthi hills. Looking north, the

67

view of the city is piteously ugly, nor is there indeed in all the plain a picturesque scene, as far as I can judge. There is a leper village here, as at Haniá and Rethymnon, outside the town. At three drew Juktas over the long endless cemetery. At the gate road we turned off — lepers as usual — through the great cemetery again, but westward, parallel with the walls. The common tall purple iris grows with great luxuriance among the tombs. 3.45 Have drawn Ida and the cemetery. (There are two lines of fort I did not perceive while drawing: thus. Also some cavy cuttings in the ditch at number 3.)

From four to five, I and George were wandering about the walls, first outside, where numberless turtledoves and the gigantic extent of the forts divided our attention, and then inside, where we got no rest from sun till we came and sat on the sea battlements. We stayed there watching the fat-tailed Anatolian sheep, the tethered horses eating green corn, etc., and then go at six. We pass Turkish soldiers exercising and observe the sergeant beat three on the head fiercely; we see promenading Levantine ladies, etc. — unlucky: out of a group darts Mr Aristárhis, His Excellency's Secretary. I said as little and seemed as stupid as I could. So we come to the place of bugs.

After a wash, I go to the 'drawing room', but the little boy has fever, and Mrs Kalokairinós is anxious. I pass my time in nursing and fussing: they say the shooting party won't come home tonight at all. Supper announced: two *scrivani* [book-keepers], Mrs Kalokairinós and Mr Harálambos. Much mishmash, and altogether a bore, though no end of kindly attention was given. At nine upstairs, and at 9.30 to bed. The stench of the *luogo* is unbearable; the squeals of a cat less so; the passing through continually of one of the ten females as much so; ditto the bugs. But my bed is a comfort for the next hour or so. 10 p.m. Dogs! cats! and O! O! the swarms of bugs!

THURSDAY 12 MAY HERAKLEION

Fifty-two years old today. Slept very tolerably. Geese, as was most fitting, loudly heralded the morning, and woke me at 4.45. Caught only 11 bugs. But the morning is cloudy, and some rain has fallen. At 5.45 I and George go on to the walls, drawing here and there bits of this impossible place, and at nine we return again towards the

Megalókastro (Herákleion), 8 a.m., 10 and 12 May.

house. No boat enlivens the dead stillness of the blue desert sea here. Hay and Moazza returned last night at midnight, having killed two rabbits. Breadeating horses. 10 At the house and from ten to eleven separating and packing some things to send back to Haniá. I buy four carpets for 650 piastres and settle accounts with Moazza for steamer. A muleteer comes also, and is ordered to go with me tomorrow at sunrise, for 15 piastres daily. Pasha Ismail paid Consul Hay a visit, 11.45. Then various bothers. Glasses of *rakí,* and dinner at twelve. The mishmashious and unclean nature of things, nine or ten women serving (one a grandmother), is amazing. Afterwards, edging in one's own affairs between consular and others, I had to ask about a muleteer, money, etc. Mr Kalokairinós brought me £20 in sovereigns, of which I pay £3 to Mr G. Kalokairinós and receive back 33 piastres change for the Rethymnon blanket — 300 piastres, and I pay 6/- to Lysimachus Kalokairinos, he giving me back 16 piastres; and £1 to Henry Moazza, who returns me 19$^1/_2$ piastres.

At three or four they went out, and I came up with George and packed the five carpets, two cloax and a bundle of shoes: a jacket, cloak, dirty linen — in two packages. It is now six, and awfully hot; truly this *is* a nasty place for smells and vermin. I went out and walked for a few minutes by the sea. George has a headache and is not himself; no wonder, having to sleep where he does. I never saw any place so full of nasty pigeonholes as this. Returned, and walked about the room. Mr Hay came back at seven; fuss and letters about his not going to a dinner he had accepted three hours ago. A *sposalizio* [engagement party] is proposed; I decline. Supper: no end of lamb and veal, and a good lobster. By persistence I get £5 changed. At 9.30 all go to the *sposalizio*. At ten I am in bed.

The weather, cloudy yesterday, is again clear and fine. Rose, 4.30, having slept tolerably, spite of bugs, of which I have only caught six. It is now 5.15 and we are utterly packed up and ready, but nobody seems up as yet, no man or mule. We had to wait and wait, in great disgust; sending and jawing and dawdling with George in the lanes by the nasty house. Hay was up also at eight, but groaning from stinx, etc. etc. At 8.45 the original muleteer came, and I can't say I like his face. I sent him with the mule to the Kainoúria Gate while I and George go round by the walls. At the gate, lo! it is not the same man but his 'brother' — one Konstandís Manosákis — whose visage is more promising. Lepers. Smart Cretans on compact trotting horses.

At 9.45 we are at the crevice and tavern of two days back. 10.45 Going up stony slope above Fortétsa. Back, the view is all cultivated, and might be Lincolnshire. 11 Descend to big bridge and Venetian aqueduct; drink good water — it runs over the bridge. Dry white and green hills. Asses and mules laden with great bales of sweet herbs for fuel. 11.15 Winding paths, pale, through herbs and heathy hillsides and a quiet upper valley of corn. 11.30 Silamos — we are near — a village; olives and corn at the foot of Juktas. Behind is the sea, and Dhia. Konstandís went this road once with a *lordhos*:[70] «Ἀλλά, μὰ τὸν Θεὸν, δὲν ἐμποροῦσε νὰ εἰπῆ μιὰν ἑλληνικὴν λέξιν· κι᾽ διὰ τοῦτο νὰ ἤτανε λόρδος, λοιπόν.» ['But, by God, he couldn't speak one word of Greek; and so he must have been a *lordhos*.']

At twelve we get to slopes of detached olives, with a pleasant gardeny village beyond, and here we fix for lunch. We sat below an olive like a Zante olive tree, and were soon well settled. Only Konstandís, a very 'smelly' man is he! — wo is me! — but when he had got some water, I and George had a good lunch on bread and meat, English cheese and good wine. The muleteer made great friends, but we thought proper that too great intimacy should not begin the first day, so we gave him three beans and *basta*. Afterwards came two men, supremely picturesque. I went above and drew till two. Some peasants passing stop, and I ask about the ruins on Juktas, which they say they never saw but «εἶναι πολὺ παλαιά» ['they are very old']. There is a church there. I wish I had seen this place by a more favourable light, 2 p.m.

We are off at 2.15 and our new guide takes us to a spring; the loveliest little *buca* [cave] possible, covered with maidenhair fern — a delicious little grot. Going uphill we come to another *metóhi*, which Konstandís calls 'Ali Bey's Metóhi': great lots of ·vine and new olives. 2.45 Ever going up: an immense green expanse. 3 p.m. More immediately below Juktas: long dry raviny hill — green — and lines of stone; wild and ugly enough. 3.15 Always up very stony sides of Juktas, but though wild there is little beauty in the scene. 3.30 Draw Mount Juktas; very Cumberlandish. (Dead ass — no, mule — by pathway.) 4 After tough ascent, rest; very Noto-ish Sicilian hills; no beauty at all.

4.15 Turn a corner and see a wide and separate valley and a really pleasant 'sparkling' neat Greek village: olives everywhere, and even with my glass I detect no ruins in this Epáno Arhánes. 4.30 Descent to valley below Arhánes: ἀηδόνια [nightingales], which our man calls «ποταμίδες» ['warblers'] — vulgar person. Their notes almost quench our thirst. Bottom of valley: stunty planes — frogs — tadpoles. Fountain, and after, a rise through narrow lanes.

5 p.m. Enquire for Konstandínos Kapládhis, and find his house at top of the village. Dark and dirty entrance; house a single room, with ladder to loft or second floor. Hearty vulgar man, squinty wife. Luggage taken down, we sit in earth-floor room, wooden alcove above. Shown in by one who says, 'Sono Ebraio io; queste son Christiani' ['I'm a Jew myself, these are Christians'], and sits down as if at home. It seems a dismal place but is but for a few hours. George asks for some coffee for me and we wait. The ever-moving Hebrew curiosity bores me. The Hebrew mizzles, which as he speaks Italian, don't displease me. Coffee comes and after, at 5.30, we all go out νὰ παρατηρήσωμε [to look at] the town.

This village is very different from those I passed above Rethymnon: the houses and people all in good order, and by comparison comfortable. One narrow alley with an arch and pergola and women sitting might have been in Italy. Mulberry trees abound. We went above the town and I drew the view, very unmolested by several who had joined us (one or two of whom merely asked to look through my glass) till 6.30. A vast yet grand scene, the dark olive groves below, and the villages — very pretty.

Returned at seven, and was the better for a wash and for a lovely nosegay of roses given me by my host who, with the hostess, is most obliging-courteous. Konstandínos Kapládhis. Odd places are these to sleep in, yet somehow I feel relieved to be here after the dreadful place at Kastro. There is no staring nor questions, though my washing must be a novelty. «Θὰ εὑρίσκεται» ['it will be found'] is the reply to my question about good wine. The supper was spread on a table, brought near, when ready, to the *divan* or wooden long seat I sit on. The supper was *snails*, herbs as salad, and παστάχι [pastáhi], this being flour and milk with oil. Host announces there is but one *trapézi* [table] so we fixed: I, George, the host and the muleteer. Crumbly-bumbly bits of loose brown bread were dealt out all over the table promiscuous by the hostess, who retired into the dark background that effort concluded. The snails, which George as well as I ate for the first time, we found really very decent, boiled in oil. The herbs in oil also were not bad, and the πάστάχι [pastáhi] capital. We all set to with small forks and the host and muleteer continually filled glasses, perpetual healths and compliments going on before and after drink; a running fire of ceremony. Wine good. After supper we declined going to 'society' at the 'café' and George began to make my bed, which incited wonder to a horrid amount, and I nearly expected to see my host lie down on it. By degrees they grew quieter, as we arranged ourselves serenely for the night, and by nine I am writing this in bed. George sleeps on a wooden dresser, on his bed; the muleteer and host in a vast square bed at the end of the room; Mrs Kapládhis upstairs with the silkworms,[71] the existence of which has prevented George smoking. As a contrast, the loveliest rosebuds, in a great jug close to me, embellish this queer scene of life.

The landscapepainter perceives the Mousfflons on the tops of the mountains of Crete

SATURDAY
14 MAY

EPANO ARHANES
KANI-KASTELLI
DHAPHNES

All things considered, I slept tolerably. There were two lights all night. Rose at 3.45 and at 4.30 I and George are ready, but Konstandís is not: that odorous youth is slow. George has smoked for a moment in the room and Mr Kapládhis exclaims about the σκουλήκια [silkworms]. O cock of the morning! Ear-splitting bird! We have sent for and paid for coffee, but the snails and asparagus, etc., and house room, are gratuitous. Off 5.20. Host, good hearty man, sees us to outside the town. Tall women — very dirty wet lane — broken aqueduct. Mists on Juktas — low — hide all.

5.45 The road, a narrow lane, execrable from great stones loose, with mud and slosh, betters as we leave the aqueduct line: varied hill and vale, olives, oax, ἀηδόνια [nightingales] — a regular garden world. 6–6.15 Leave this richly-wooded valley and begin to round the end of Juktas, over pleasant sandy greeny hill. 6.15 Descend wild hilly district; goats. End of Juktas all rocky; view beyond all hilly-greeny. 6.20 See Ida, and the chain of mountain, beyond the rox of Juktas; also double-headed Kani-

72

Kastélli. Stop and draw till seven, a grand mountain scene. Birds calling, mists floating.

7.30 Stony wide ravine hill scenes. 8 I stop and draw Juktas, which is very grand here, but I am amazed to find *all* Crete is mountain. Do not feel well, and am undecided about going far on this journey.

8.45 More rock and ravine, ascents and descents, bring us to near Kani-Kastélli, below the fortress rock of which we sit and rest, while Konstandís goes down to a spring for water.

9.30 The water was good, and we went up to Kani-Kastélli, a miserable place half full of ruined houses, below the old fort rock. Here we got some wine at a shop. The people were civil — Mussulmen mostly — but rough. 9.45–10 Going down to the Triton: scenery unwieldy, with huge lines of green hill and, above, the Ida range. We go down to nearly the bottom of the valley, and sit below a large plane, where (a bore) two men with guns join us. People here seem to think it rude to leave one alone. The wineshop above was dirty and dark and the place unsatisfactory. At ten the two *cacciatori* [hunters], who had been joined by two others, left, and we began to dine, having asked Konstandís the muleteer 'to dinner', as he seems a quiet creature; and it would be a shame to eat at the expense of these people daily — said muleteer being one of the party — and not ask him to be one of ours. Our dinner was bread and cold beefy veal, cheese, onions and watercresses (George's find in the stream) and very good wine, though too sweet (bought two bottles for three piastres!), of Kani-Kastélli. It is now 11.30, the muleteer sleeps and George is gone insect and flower hunting. The wavy plane shade is delightful and the myriad warble-twitter of birds wondrous and lovely: larks, titmice and all Twitterers. It seems to me I am at Peppering forty years ago, and trains of thought 'arise in me'.[72] Last night George made a vain effort to get me some food alone: 'It would be shameful to leave him so,' said the host, 'alone he must never eat.' 'But', says George (repeating the scene to me), 'my master is one humble man; he wants no company — but they would not let me say so.' 12.30 Somewhat have we slept. 1.30 We are going to start. What a bright birdy green scene! — a single huge plane the only object in the foreground.

At two, having descended to a lonely corn-growing ravine, we ford a small river (Triton). 2.45 At the top of a very long and hot ascent — and yet not quite at top — opposite our dinner plane tree. No good to be got out of any of these views, and I greatly incline to go back to Kastro by the Monday's steamer. At three rest a good deal: unwell, and almost resolve to return. 3.30 Dhaphnés in sight, a large village in a low bottom; Aghios Myron beyond. But the scene is woody and beautiful (or Claude-like): all blue and green — Swiss. At 4.30 I have drawn it, and have sent in Konstandís, who has sent out some water; and I go on.

At 4.40 we reach Kyrios Manuél Bernardhákis his house: a low place in a small courtyard, half an earth floor as usual, half a raised platform, in this case hung round with carpets and cotton wares. Beyond, a room-cellar full of vats of oil and wine, and beyond that again a small garden. Glad I was of water and coffee, and I took three quinine pills at once. I and George both think it better that I should give up farther journeys in Crete: first, the advanced season and increasing heat; second, the little picturesqueness gained by so much toil; third, the bad food and dirt and the little rest — are all good reasons for leaving Crete. We go and sit in the small garden yard. Mr Bernardhákis, who is a small old deaf Cerigotto, gives me stocks and roses, wine and uneatable biscuit knobs. George falls to gathering herbs, and Konstandís washes his feet and puts on shoes. Sitting to draw in the hot sun knocks one into nothing. Mrs Bernardhákis is a pleasing woman, and there is a shy but handsome daughter. The view from this place is very *foody*: green and blue, but sadly wanting in form.

The evening is a bore. Fleas endless. The old host deaf, inquisitive, tiresome-foolish. «Ἔχετε πατάτες; Ἔχετε ἐκκλησίες; Ἀκόμη πολεμοῦν στὴν Ἀμερική;» ['Do you have potatoes? Do you have churches? Are they still fighting in America?'] and so on. How this night is to be passed, far less ten others, I don't know. We did not get supper till eight: *good* rice soup, tough fowl, tough artichokes and a sort of omelette. I ate as little as I could, the old cove being particularly nasty and a bore. The amount of salutations before and after drinking are wonderful.

9.45 I have never known any travelling so hard as this in Crete. The muleteer was desired to go to another house, and went away sulky: the hostess says, «Διότι ἔχω ἕνα παιδάκι θηλυκό.» ['Because I have a female child.'] No possibility of *luogo*, or of *po*, and the dreadful coughing old man is going to sleep in this room, which is so disposed: [plan]. We have three lamps alight, but then the stinx are sublime and various. Always I am covered with fleas. Bother travels in Crete.

SUNDAY
15 MAY

DHAPHNES
VENERATO
EVGHENIKI
AGHIOS THOMAS

It is 4.30 and we two are ready. I slept better than I had expected. The old man made less noise than might be, and the cats didn't come in. I have taken a magnesia draught, and two quinine pills are to follow. So, after all, I determine to go ahead. The return to Kastro would be too shocking, and almost as bad as a fever in itself. I and George debate about it. The old man and wife give me flowers, the daughter is good-looking, but all muddle and poke about and worry. Also there are cockroaches, as well as bugs and fleas. We confer about paying and Konstandís avers 15 piastres to be just. The difficulty of getting at anything in these crowded holes! After all, they do all they can — filthy as that is — to put themselves out of the way for me. And the old Manuél Bernardhákis is a cheery old chap, although so deaf and dirty. He remembers Vido[73] with olive trees, and when there was no water in Corfu city: but his leanings are evidently French.

Off at five. Form of the hill of Aghios Myron good. The mule looks back to her home — like Lot's wife. Doubtless snow would improve the hills on the right. Corn, corn. Anatolian sheep. Wide, gulfy, shadeless hills, hiding Ida. Light mists, no sun. Great cultivation. Two villages, plains of corn narrow. 5.45 Medicine works. Quinine. Vineyard and olives.

6 Stop at *khan* and have *rakí*. Well-dressed fine people. 6.15 Draw Veneráto: lonely and grand scene. Nightingales! Pass village — Evghenikí — right; Kerása was left

74

Veneráto, 6.15 a.m., 15 May.

below. Most lovely green undrawable vales! 6.30 Leave high road to Messará. Lovely leafy thickets and glens! Birds! birds! birds! Plane — stream — fine olives — lovely lanes. 6.45 Up rocky hill, whence are good views of villages and Aghios Myron beyond; fertile, gay and beautiful. 7 Leave shady lanes, and emerge on bare hills, save for heath and corn. Long wide rolling view of mountains eastward: Juktas long and somewhat like Gennaro [in Sicily]. 7.30 Up till now rounding a bare hill, higher and higher, by a narrow edgy path, and draw till eight, an expanse of view. Shortly after turning the hill, gray rocks and oakwoods fill up the higher end of the valley, and above the extreme end is Aghios Thomás, where we are going. The path up to it is quite delightful for thick verdure and two or three tumbling streams. Gardens: oaks, cherries, etc. etc. We look for a place to settle in for the day and taking out George's bed and my saddlebag send Konstandís and the mule on to the town. I get out Pashley, and by degrees change everything: shirt, drawers and socks. But hardly are those I take off put into the bag, than two men come and sit and stare.

It is now ten, and only one bore remains. After that old creature went I reposed in the shade, and at eleven George and I had lunch or dinner, removing our traps to an oak tree farther from the path. The vast multitude of blackbirds, nightingales and

Aghios Thomás, 4.30 p.m., 15 May.

many other sorts of birds is wonderful and most delightful, as is this mountain scene: sitting below oaks, a cornfield sloping down to the stream and to thick groves of walnut and cherry; above these, opposite to where I lie, rises a steep hill, slanting off into a summit of rox, but the sides are covered with plane, walnut, olive and oak, cornfields, and here and there rocks and a few cypresses. Far off, the cawing of rooks, which brings back days — 'days that are no more' — so long gone as those of 1823, when I first heard the voice of rooks in Sussex .... 'O life! O earth! O time! On whose last steps . . .' .[74] It is noon, and considering how unwell I was yesterday, happiness abounds. The sun-loving cistus gleams rosily. We incline to sleep, but Konstandís and three friends come and sit, presenting white and red roses; three more follow, but finding us immovably averse to converse, flee. (Blackbird = κοτσύφι.) 1 p.m. The longer one looks at this place the lovelier it seems. 1.30 I walk to rocks above, just by the town, and find a glorious scene, which is much to say in Crete. A kind of sadness — 'tears, idle tears' — comes over me, so much here reminds me of England, and of other days.

It is now 3.30 and I wish Konstandís would come, or that I was as little liable to [illegible] thought as George is.

However, at 3.45 came the punctual Konstandís, and I and George leaving him to take the rest of the traps we went to the place I had been up to, wot looks down over the birthplace of Minerva and the burial place of Jupiter. (It was hot enough there yesterday to split anybody's head.) (They call the fogs or mists here ἀντάρα [andára]: ὁμίχλαι [omíhlai] in Corfu.) Few scenes can be grander or fresher than this. Here, several of the villagers came, all very plain and kindly, and one — my host of tonight (the Ἀναγνώστης [Lay Reader]) — a fine stout fellow. All laughed at my taking a portrait of one of the lot, and all stand near till I had done at 4.30, and then accompanied me to a spot higher up, where I drew the scene: still finer as to a foreground of vast rox and oax, but blotted out by clouds as to distance. It was cool, so at 5.30 I moved with my suite to the village, a place full of ruins, built among rox, containing 80 houses now — 300 once. (Arhánes has 300 *now;* Dhaphnés 80.) Having passed lots of 'stony places' and groups of respectfully rising and saluting peasants, we came to a courtyard, wondrous as to cleanness, and going up the usual parapetless stairs, lo! a room nearly as large as my Corfu studio, with neat sofas and *absolutely* clean. The effect was stunning, and increased by the entrance of a Lady in (a crinoline?) pale muslin, extremely like Lady Stratford.[75] Amazement! And later her mother, and two small children. Two other men besides my host were there, and we talked of nightingales (who never leave Crete but breed here), of swallows (who go in October), of the Queen of India, London and many other matters. 'But why did you destroy the Ionian fortresses?' «Δέν ἐξεύρω τίποτε διὰ τοῦτα τὰ πράγματα» ['I don't know anything about such things'], said I, which abolished that line of talk.

After washing, having been left alone for once, about 7.30 I was called to a room below, where the host, wife and mother, I, George and Konstandís made up a table. Good rice soup, boiled fowl, cheese, and cherries and excellent wine: the whole cleanly and with no show — bar the usual cumbrous Cretan healths — plainly, and in very decent order. Contrasted with last night we are in Paradise. Bed at nine or earlier in the large room.

Aghios Thomás, 5 a.m., 16 May.

MONDAY
16 MAY

AGHIOS THOMAS
MEGALI VRISI
VOURVOULITIS
MOULIA
AGHII DHEKA

George unwell — cherries, to wit — all night. He and I go out at five, leaving *roba* and Konstandís to follow. He says Konstandís says the Ἀναγνώστης [Lay Reader] said no at first, but took the 20 piastres graciously. I sit to draw among the great rox, which at Aghios Thomás are magnificently picturesque. Oddly enough, George remembers some similar rox and ivy in some of Penry Williams's paintings,[76] and says, 'Si il Signor Guglielmo era qui aveva assai di fare.' ['If Signor Williams were here he would have enough to do.']

5.45 Have made a drawing; position very superb and rox vastly grand. Off, across a pleasant green flat or small plain. Hooded crows. Nice well-behaved peasants.

Pass Prevelianá, left. 6 Pleasant olives, corn and oax. Fine cows. 6.15 Pass through Megali Vrisi, a very ruinous tumbledown village. Old man said, 'What do you sell?' (a constant query on the road).

«Παιγνίδια» ['toys'], says Konstandís.

'Let me see them.'

'No, not here — in the village.'

78

So the old man followed and when in the village close by, Konstandís laughed at him, as did all the other villagers immensely.

«Κανείς ποτέ μὲ περιγέλασε ὥς ἐσέ!» ['Nobody ever made such a fool of me as you!'] said the rustic.

6.30 Passing over high tableland — undulating — corn — southern range of mountains in sight, beyond the end of Ida chain. Metóhi Aghia Pelaghía on the right. Larks. At seven, lo! the plain of Messará — east; the cumbrous lower Ida chain — west. 7.30 The plain of Messará increases in interest, but is not eminently beautiful. A long and wide plain, somewhat like the Bekaa [in the Lebanon], but wanting its decision of colour, form and lines: here, all is green endless undulations, barring one flat space below long and not very lovely hill ranges. However, such as it is, I draw it, and start again at eight. The morning is hot, but with fine air.

The Messará plain was in sight, till lower hills began to be crossed, ever more or less covered with corn, and so we came, by nine, to a scanty olive patch below a little Ottoman village called Vourvoulítis. There is not much shade, and as is usual in these cases irretrievably ugly: indeed a more uninteresting three hours' walk I never took, barring the sight of the plain, and that is not a very remarkable matter. If possible, I shall certainly get to Halépa by Wednesday or Thursday week.

The scanty olive patch is grateful. George would make up his bed for me, and he and Konstandís are about to join the 'midday repast'. Two Othomaní have brought us a μυζήθρα [mizíthra] cheese (ricotta called in long-past Roman days) which we buy for 6 piastres (1/-) — and as it will last three days that ain't dear. The Turx seem quiet good sort of folk. We passed a village, Moulia, of Othomaní, not long before we reached this. I am writing now, at 11.30, and we have had our lunch of eggs, Guarracino and μυζήθρα [mizíthra] cheese, bread and wine, and George, after long discourse on Ceylon and elephants, has gone to sleep, as Konstandís has done a good while since. The Suliot snores, which for once I allow, as he had no sleep last night. He is disgusted that the Aghios Thomás host put water in our wine; not so I, as I wanted to drink a great deal, being thirsty. The she-mule, an amazing beast for leaping over walls with a backful of luggage, flaps her tail and is woodenly tranquil. The wine was, certainly, utterly diluted: we drank it out of the foot of the candlestick, which, like my tin cup, is broken. Last night's lodgings were wonderfully *clean*, quite unlike any that I have yet seen in Crete, except Hay's house. And Mrs Ἀναγνώστης [Lay Reader] was so absurdly like Lady Stratford that I have doubt still if it were not Lady S. disguised. Birds as usual abound here: some blackbirds, no ἀηδόνια [nightingales] (though I learn that they build and rear young at Aghios Thomás), tomtits, and larks. It is quite cloudy now and breezy, and as we are on high ground, pleasant truly. The Othomaní, however, don't come and bore one as the Kritikí [Cretans] are wont to do. It is 11.45. The gray clouds seem very English. They are gathering mulberry leaves «διὰ τὰ σκουλήκια» ['for the silkworms']. Security to wit: we lie with all our traps, beds, *bisacchi* [saddlebags], and money around, no-one dreaming of hurting us. The singular want of southern — or eastern — vegetation is constantly most noticeable.

George being asleep, Konstandís has come to talk about distances, and has improved the opportunity by adding, «῎Aς πᾶμε.» ['Let's go.'] There are three or four hours to go from here to Aghii Dheka, and it is cloudy and no sun. Moreover, it is doubtful if any drawings can be made. Say I, 'If we go now, we arrive at three or four and our present *topos* [place] is *kalós* [good]'; «Εὐτυχοί εἴμαστε ἐδῶ· διατί νὰ ἀναχωρήσωμεν;» ['We're happy here; why should we leave?']; it is better to sleep awhile. So Konstandís turns round, saying a low «καλά» ['very well'] and instantly lies down and goes to sleep. Obedience is a virtue. So, both my followers are asleep.

(Ah! J. D. Harding! I could have liked once more to have seen you! Wide apart as we were in all thought, yet you had some astonishingly true and original perceptions: and moreover I owed you for some benefits. I write this because I am recollecting some of J. D. H.'s illustrations of Lord Byron. Also I am feeling that I have received — not much personally — but much through Gale and Fowler; advantages of which I [illegible] and acknowledge the value far more now than then, and which I regret I never showed a wish to repay.)[77]

(Worthy of the foulest of fanatics, be they of Mahomet, Papal, or the *Record*.)[78]

A number of villagers come to us later and are very harmless, though more or less a bore. One, however, makes such a row that I put on my boots to go; nor is George pleased with their playing with long knives. At 2–2.15 we linger. 2.30 We have started, and anything more hideous than the long wrinkled hills with scraps of purple above them, clouded and gray, can't be. Ugh! winding ever over dry weary hills. 2.45 We come in sight — so to speak — of the southern sea, only it is not visible for cloud, barring one island called Paximádhi ['Rusk']. Konstandís, on our joking about dry bread, throws us into fits by saying it is an *island*, and not bread, etc. etc. etc.

3 p.m. After endless weary beastly ugliness, we seem to be coming again near the plain of Messará — at Gortyn, or nearly so. Descent by an ugly pathed narrow gorge of frightful hill. 3.15 Most hideous gorge! A pile of sliding stones and earth on each side, and no outlet of picturesque or grand whatever, and all covered with gray cloud: a bad Westmoreland pass. 3.30 We are out of the gorge and near on the plain, which for extent of corn and cultivation seems to me only exceeded by the Bekaa. But the lines about it are so commonplace and dull, as is the sky, that draw it I can *knot*. However, I *did* draw later, inasmuch as I might never get any other view of this place; and having done so, we make for the village of Aghii Dheka, a total-miserable scrubby collection of narrow ways between half or wholly ruined houses of one storey high. Lots of old columns, friezes, etc. etc. about.[79] At 4.15 we were at Captain Elías's house — O Lord! what a falling-off from expectation was there! — or from Aghios Thomás! A vastly dark beastly hole (the upper half of the house, reached by the usual ladder) is being cleaned out by a woman (daughter-in-law of Captain Elías): a forlorn place and wretched. George and I sit on the top of part of the house, and George says the room is so full of silkworms we can hardly sleep in it. Konstandís having to get a saddle mended, has gone to Mitrópolis, and if possible is to procure some wine, as there is literally nothing here but dry stale bread. Old Elías, who received Pashley in 183[4],

is out at a mill. Pomegranates abound. Turkish cemeteries also, though there are only a few — three or four — Ottoman families live here now. Captain Elías's son and I converse: concerning silkworms; concerning his mother, who died ten days ago; concerning his brother, who has murdered a man and fled; and concerning antiquities: said son being very filthy indeed. 5.30 It is too late to go out and draw now, and is all but raining. So we walk about on the tremulous tops of several houses and observe various filthiness and ruin, which it seems to me is the greatest characteristic of Gortyn. Yet there are signs of beauty in the inequalities of ground on the distant plain, and in the olive groups and the scattered masses of ruin which I see with my glass.

(Three new things I have done, never before done in all my life: first, to drink wine out of a candlestick; second, to sup on snails; third, to walk for two hours on the tops of houses.) Konstandís comes, bringing wine, and lo! at six it rains!

6.30 It did not rain long, but we still sit on housetops, Konstandís having joined the party, and I go in from time to time to see the silkworms, which are in three batches. Old Captain Elías, who has come, is a very different man from what you would expect his foul abode to manifest: a gentleman in manner and feeling, tall and the remains of a very fine man — he is about 65 — but with a great shade of melancholy, which the death of his wife and flight of his son, besides that he has a deaf and dumb son also, are enough to account for. (The deaf and dumb son's wife has also just died.) Aghii Dheka is I fancy a very unhealthy place, and all the villagers look pale and yellow. The supper was uncouth and nasty to the last degree. O that supper!

which even George could hardly bear: the smallest of round tables had to serve for myself, George, Konstandís, the old man and his son; the woman strewed every spot on it with watered bread. Rice soup (I had the honour of a basin to myself) and a boiled fowl (which had to be held for want of room and for fear of cats), which all clawed up instantly, George only having the presence of mind to secure me some in my basin. Μυζηθρόπηττες [cheese pies] afterwards, and Konstandís did the honours of the wine. Nor was there scarcely any room to sit or move, along of the silkworms. A queerer and filthier arrangement could hardly be found in mid-Africa. After the δεῖπνον [supper] we sat talking on the houseroof, to make the night as short as possible. Captain Elías hardly recalls Pashley, though he has known very many travelling with Maniás [Pashley's guide]. Poor Captain Elías: he seemed to know all the current news: Danish, American, Greek, etc. And when George had gone in to make the bed he tapped me and said, «Πότε θὰ ἐλευθερωθῇ ἡ δυστυχής πατρίδα μας; Ἐσὺ ἐξερεύεις, ἐξερεύεις καλά — ἀλλά πότε;» ['When will our unhappy country be freed? You know; you know very well — but when?'] To which I could only reply, «Ποιός ἐξερεύει; Ἴσως μιὰν ἡμέραν.» ['Who knows? Perhaps one day.'] By nine George had made my bed, and we all retired to this remarkable kennel. It is now 9.30. [Plan of room.] The live macaroni-like silkworms are far from pleasant, and I don't know how I shall get through the night.

TUESDAY
17 MAY

AGHII DHEKA
GORTYN
AMBELOUZO
POBIA

All things being done on the housetop, we are ready thereon at 4.30. For one was glad — fleas, flies, bugs, ants, swallows, silkworms, dogs, cats and cocks considered — to rise at 3.30. This is the worst hole I have slept in in Crete, *senza dubbio*. Leaving Konstandís and luggage, I, George, and Captain Elías went out at 4.45 from the poor village westward toward Mitrópolis and Ambeloúzo. All the plain is covered with great or small masses of ruins: masses of Roman rubble, and brickwork and columns, etc. At the theatre, several portions of which are standing, I drew till six: the view of the plain is beautiful thence, and greatly pleased me. But it began to rain (!) for the morning is very cloudy: and earwigs and fleas provoked me. So I went on to the ruined Cathedral of St Titus with Captain Elías and then left him, poor man, giving him 25 piastres. There is something about him that wrings the heart: quiet suffering. I drew, on the other side of a stream, above, on what seems to have been a lower acropolis (for the whole of two or three spurs of the mountains are covered with remains of buildings) till 7.15. Stopped by heavier rain showers. Desolate yet beautiful spot!

7.30 George, Konstandís and the mule join me, and I go on, over the beautiful plain: reaping corn — heavy shower of rain — clear again — fine cattle. 7.40 Reach Ambeloúzo, where there are plane trees, but the village is much like Aghii Dheka. Send Konstandís into the village to know if Captain Korakas has arrived. Rain ceases, and clouds rise. 7.45 The Captain is not come, so we go down to the plain, from the edge of it where we now are. The extent of ruined city is immense and one sees, looking back, the two acropolis-like hills, all over remains and walls.

8 We are in sight of the Monastery of Pesanés on the opposite hills.

9 Ever the plain: mountains finer. We pass river (the Gheropotamós-Lithaío), a wide stony torrent, but with little water now. 9.15 Arrive at cave and spring of water and we intend, only it rains continually, to lunch a little farther up the hill. 9.30 Preliminary retreat to rox; strip, and catch nine large live fleas and three dead. Return to lunch, of three courses: 1. Hard eggs cum onions. 2. Bread and Cheshire cheese 3. *Ricotta* and sugar and wine. And as the sun was hidden behind a cloud, we were

Gortyn, 7–8 a.m., 17 May.

very comfortable, although not below trees. It is now 11.30. My two comrades sleep. 'I, only I `awake', etc.[80] Contrary to xpectation, my health is good. The plain is — as it is: ἔτσι κ' ἔτσι [so-so]. The hills are dark purple, but they were better in this shower and cloud than clear.

1.30 Time has passed by overhauling all my saddlebag, making two drawings, arranging those already made, wandering and wobbling about. 2 p.m. We are packing the *fortómata* [baggage] and are about to go. Alas, it recommences to rain. 2.20 Pass, left, Peri; and somewhat further on, left also, Alithiní: both seedy scattery villages. 3 Going slowly up back hills, not pretty at all. Sky all cloudy and gray, and dropping showers at times. One sees well hence the princely position of Gortyn. 3.15 It comes on to rain so hard that we all stop below an olive tree. 3.50 We reach Pobia, a large village with no end of archy doors and broken walls, overlooking the plain, and at the top are met by Mrs Korakas; their house, into which she receives us, being the highest in the village. As usual, one lower long room, in this particular instance divided off into a higher portion for a store and kitchen, both — or rather, all one — very low;

Pobia, 5–6 p.m., 17 May.

beyond, a ladder leading to the dark low chamber above. Sweets and coffee were very refreshing. Presently Captain Michael Korakas came: the big hearty man I saw at Kastro. The rest of the afternoon I spent in trying to draw, but nearly constant rain prevented me, though by hard effort by sunset I succeeded in getting a view of Ida and the plain, the former being from here very fine. It is now 6.30, *so cold* and so windy I must go inside, tormented though I be with fleas. 9 p.m. I write in bed. Nothing, except the flies and fleas, has been unpleasant here. After a wash in the upper room, which is hung with arms and carpets etc. etc., the table was set before Captain Michael Korakas and me, George and Konstandís. Good rice soup and boiled fowl, olives, *dolmás*, and salad, $\mu\nu\zeta\dot{\eta}\theta\rho\alpha$ [mizíthra cheese], oranges in quarters sugared and Aghios Myron wine made a supper for a king. Captain Michael continually drank the health of the Queen and Hay as well as of Lysimachus Kalokairinós and we talked of the villages on the road etc. to Sphakiá. He is not easy to understand, but as far as I can judge one may go there or anywhere else one likes; but I don't get any more definite idea about particular places or persons. The supper was cleanly and orderly and a pleasant contrast to that of last night. *En revanche* there came, if possible, *more*

84

Pobia, 6 a.m., 18 May.

fleas. Order of sleeping is thus [plan] in the good-sized upper room. Lo! the host comes, and turns into Konstandís' mattress! So be it. Wind howls. (At the same moment which her Papa undresses, enter daughter with a glass of water for me.) This is the fifth night of 'Cretan travel'. I fear fleas will prevent all sleep.

The love of the island is immensely noticeable in all Cretans: «Πῶς σοῦ φαίνεται ἡ νῆσος μας, ἡ πατρίδα μας;» ['What do you think of our island, our country?']

Up by four, but we are to wait for bread being made. Sky all gray and cloudy, Londonwise. Carpets shown — Miss Korakas' work. We go up with Captain Korakas to a height and behold Ida and the plain and draw, and return to the house by 5.30. Captain Korakas asks for a coffee mill. (He has suddenly begun to comb his head close by me.) This waiting for bread is a horrid bore, as it is now nearly 6.30. Happily, the morning is cool. 6.40 The mule is brought and Konstandís has swept her all over with a broom. The bread is made and out-taken. I give two pencils to Aristídhis and one to Stelianós. Costume here: red fez, red handkerchief and girdle; all rest dark blue, and tan boots. At seven we set off down towards the plain, Ida being pretty clear but all other hills, and the sky, clouded. George growls that Mrs Korakas asked him apart to ask me to send something for her daughter's dower to Haniá, and various

WEDNESDAY
18 MAY

POBIA
[PHAESTOS]
TYMBAKI
KLIMA
SATA
VATHIAKO
APODHOULOU

85

other matters. Captain Korakas accompanied me out of the town. At 7.30 drew: beautiful Claude-like olive scenes. One peasant, yellow boots. Met several armed men riding. Petrokepháli, 8.10–8.15, a horrid decayed village but with superb pomegranate and other gardens. Ever a dusty broad flat road. 9 Rain. Some fine dells, and Ida above. Olives. Pass Aghios Ioánnis, right; apparently small, but not so. Pass through it. *Festa:* idle people. 9.15 Hard rain, and obliged to halt below an olive. I could not draw Ida at any time during the walk, as it was clouded directly I got to the plain: yet some scenes were evidently beautiful. 9.45 Weather holds up, and we go on, meeting many peasants, red, black and blue, and we went out at the end of all Messará, when lo! *pouring* rain! Shelter again, after having crossed two small rivers, one of which George helped me to cross on stones, and I nearly fell in. We were nearly wet through by the heavy rain before we got to the tree. Rain stops. Mule behaves odiously. Fierce dog — exception in Crete. Tall olives. Bright sun. Long fields of olives and corn. Savage dog, single Cretan exception. Arrive at 10.45 at Tymbáki, a miserable but large space of flat boxy houses, with more hens and naked children than can be imagined. Neither is the air good here, so I thought it better to go on, at almost any risk, to Apodhoúlou, and ἀποφάσισα [I decided] that much. For there was no good at all in staying at the town, although various good people have said Tymbáki is a 'large village', 'a fine village', 'the best place in these parts' — yet, knowing the Cretan world, I doubted, and with justice it seems; for a more filthy hole — or holes, as it is full of holes — cannot be. So, asking the way of a peasant, Konstandís took us, threading the way through the angular circular and narrow lanes, and at last coming out on the leanly olive-clad flat ground outside. Konstandís got the basin filled with water at one of the houses and brought it out some way, and there, below some very Raphaelesque olive trees, we sat down. Ida had been perfectly clear after that violent rain, yet fearing cloud might arise I gave up all thoughts of food — 11.15 — and set to work at once to make a drawing, having, in order to do so, to go a considerable way off, when lo! clouds riz at once and no Ida was any more visible! Would I had made drawings earlier today! Yet that could not be. Verily fortune smiles not on this Ida trip. So I went back to George and Konstandís and we ordained lunch, though at first not comfortably as a great wind arose and only large stones could keep things in their places. Nevertheless, we lunched on eggs, bread and cheese, μυζήθρα [mizíthra] cum sugar, and totally astonishing wine of Aghios Myron. It is now 12.40. How the wind sweeps over the plain! The coast is not beautiful. It is nearly one and we are packing. (Why do Dr and Mrs Dunn, the Danses and other early fooly people come before me now?)[81] Meanwhile, clouds hide all mountains, and Ida might be Penmaenmawr for aught I see. Off at one, over the plain and then rising towards Ida *(always hidden)*, and so up — up — up — till we are now — 2 p.m. — far aloft and overlooking the plain and sea and Paximádhi. The sea is blue, the coast is bosh: there is nothing to draw. But there is a good breeze, and now — two — we will go on.

2.30 Always such a going up. Stop till 2.40 and draw Paximádhi: a very uninteresting view. At three we are over the southward-looking hill, and see a vast valley, Sata village only therein, and olives. Snow Ida-line above. Kedros left. Down hill (I omitted stopping at [Klima?] where we got some water).

Wide, fine, but gloomy and *piuttosto* commonplace mountain scenery. But Sata — 3.35 — is in a grand quiet verdant mountain valley.

Mount Ida (a painting based on drawings made on 24 and 25 May).

4 Alas! Alas! green as is the scene and fresh the air, I am sad and cross, having been angry for half an hour (along of Konstandís stealing artichokes, which I seized and threw away), and of being wholly and totally disgusted. We dip into vast deep valleys, and are to ascend great hills, but I brood over leaving Crete the very soonest possible. At 5.15 after tremendous pulls, passing another ruinous village (Vathiakó), we got to Apodhoúlou, which doubtless contains more or less picturesque, but somehow it was impossible to draw it. In the village, at a wineshop where several Mussulmen were quarrelling, a man in Levantine garments, a hat, etc., was pointed out to me as the son of Aléxandros, and so it turned out: Mrs Hay's nephew.[82] He seemed to make me very welcome, but one of the Mussulmen *would* make him and me drink, and the scene was not pretty. We were taken to the *konak* [staging-post], a stout well-built house, but all uncared for, and we sat in an open gallery, into which shortly came two quite drunken Moslim, one with four glasses, two of which he let fall and, they broken, he returned with shame whence he came. The host talked a good deal of his uncle and aunt Hay, who are sixty — he — and she fifty years old: showed me a

87

seal, crest goat (as below) [sketch], and a watch, all broken more or less. This young man is an intelligent fellow, though utterly dirty and neglected. He has a school of 40 children from the village and other villages who sit, some of them shirtless and most shoeless, in what was I suppose the drawing room. Another brother is here, and their father, whom I took for a Moslim — Mrs Hay's brother (not John, who is in Egypt, nor Konstantin, who is dead). We sat in the gallery, and the two drunken Turks made themselves asses. Later, we were put into what was once the bedroom, where some good articles of furniture still spoke of other days of wealth and comfort. Then came 'supper': eggs and a rice pilaf, which George had made; George is never out of humour, though tonight sorely tried by the dirt and *scomodi modi* [inconvenient ways] of our dwelling. Artichokes also there were, but the extreme filth of the whole was hideous; so, George having made my bed, we shut up for the night — the muleteer being already asleep — if only to avoid the whole village which had come into the gallery to stare at me, and began to crowd the room. The house is an example of misplaced expense — a ruin. Chairs, a bed and good English bolts, locks, etc. etc. etc., but every part decayed and in the hands of savages. Rabbits, a goat, swallows, etc., rush and flit about the rooms. Part of this is written on the morning of the 19th, which is clear and lovely, and we are up by four.

THURSDAY
19 MAY

APODHOULOU
MONASTERY OF
ASOMATOS
MONASTERY OF
ARKADHI

«Αμισφιλδ» [Amisfield, in East Lothian] is the only address of Mr Hay I can get, but it is known to George Kalokairinós. Off at six, having made a drawing of the house from above, accompanied by Phanoúrios. Very lovely morning. Poor good people! they are half savage. Ida is seen, but by no means pleases me: dome-like, and too near. Very probably from the road to Preveli, it would be finer, but then hardly ever clear. As things are, Haniá is my aim.

7.15 We are stopping, along of the luggage falling, Konstandís having whacked the mule, which jumped and shook off articles. The route has been between Ida — an ugly dome — and immense green valleys, olive dotted: not a scrap to draw; great ascent and descent to Amári Kastélli — fine valley — Ida more drawable now, but of course has become clouded, 8.45.

'Gheórghios Saounátis — Manouél Saounátis of Rethymnon': name of man at a roadside *khan* where we stop and have some good wine at 9–9.15. (A sort of general shop, and I buy a bridle.) Good Aghios Myron wine costs 200 to 250 piastres — the barrel, which is 100 or 150 *okádhes*.

Pleasant walk. Ἀηδόνια [nightingales]. Myrtles, great size; always a very rich yellow green. Clouds increasing. Meronas and other villages, all of which Konstandís knows the names of. They make much silk. Ida always covered, the truth being that she is unwilling to have comparisons made by a distinguished landscape-painter.

10 Going through great olive groves, all property of the Monastery of Asómatos, at which George says he is sure they will say they are poor and have only two eggs. George also bursts out resolving to buy a fish at Haniá, and to roast it himself without oil. 10.30.

10.45 We arrive at the Monastery of Asómatos, but are sorrily received in a dirty bare room and by very dirty lay *kalógheri*. As nobody came, and as they said the *Hegoúmenos* was just going off to Preveli, I thought fit after 20 or 25 minutes to send the Pasha's letter, which speedily brought the *Hegoúmenos;* but he was a man of no appearance of manner or friendliness, while the other clown *kalógheros* sat staring and yawning. Nothing being said, except a suggestion that Arkádhi was near, I asked for something to eat, when the *Hegoúmenos* said, 'Have you not eaten today?' and shortly after he went away. Presently they brought us a small plate of stewed pigeon, one of eggs, and one of nasty πάστάχι [pastáhi] with a sweet wine — not very good — and we three sat down to make the best of it. At the present moment, noon, we have made our lunch, and the *Hegoúmenos* has made his adieux, and the clown giant lay monx have tumbled down the ladder: a rather scurvy lot. I have decided to go to Arkádhi, for the head man going away, and faring as we do so ill while he is here, what should we do when he is gone? So, we are to repoge till 1 p.m. It must be said, George's attention and activity are the greatest comforts. Coffee has since been brought, but so bad as to be undrinkable. And the worst of all is, the mountain is always wholly covered, so that here, where naturally the views of Ida would be the finest, not a line can I draw. O churly monx! At one, I wake George and Konstandís and lo! whereas they were both of accord before, i.e., that it is better to go than to stay, now they hesitate. Konstandís says it is very far, and will rain: George says the mule will suffer. George says pay nothing: I think it better to pay something. Off at 1.20, cloudy all. Ida hidden. Myrtle thickets. Ἀηδόνια [nightingales]. Richly wooded slopes of Ida — headless Ida. 2.20 Terminate ascent, and begin descent. Always huge rich valleys. No, ascent *not* finished: begins again, and goes on to 2.45. Descent sharp till three. Fountain of the 'Stone' very cold. Konstandís says no one drinks of it. Ascend again, 3.5–3.45: long pull. Leave track to Rethymnon and turn to the right. All gray fog and mist.

3.55 at top — all mist — Arkádhi just visible. We sit and smoke till four. Plain. Pines. Arkádhi at 4.50: fog, almost a small mizzly rain. It is now six, and I am glad to have come here for the *Hegoúmenos* is a very jolly man and hearty, and gave us all sweets, water, coffee and *rakí* in no time. Also I am well washed, and comparatively comfortable. The place seems picturesque but the dark mizzling fog prevents one seeing much. Fleas commence. How to get back to Halépa by Sunday or Monday? George's good humour is always a blessing, and when they brought coffee for me and for him only, he instantly gave half to the muleteer, of his, tired as he was. (This morning, returning to the house at Apodhoúlou for my small box of flea powder, I found Aléxandros and others taking snuff out of it, as they thought!) The name of the *Hegoúmenos* here is Gabriel. There was a long waiting and semi-sleep before supper, which happened at 7.30 in a very remote room. The Gabriel, who is a man of the world, was very jolly and pleasant and apologized, unnecessarily, for the supper, owing to its late coming: stewed pigeons, three sorts of salad, a dish of honey, cherries, beans, cheese, etc. etc. and with very good wine, though a little too sweet. Everything was orderly and hearty. Healths, Cretan fashion, abundant. Afterwards, coffee and

The church and courtyard of the Monastery of Arkádhi (from Pashley's *Travels in Crete*).

smoking. It seems that the walls of the church and monastery are thick as ever; only the inside was burned in 1823. Gabriel has been at Jerusalem, and that fact was a great gain for George and me, *qua* conversation. At nine we retired; I, I am sorry to say, to a square room with no outlet whatever, and though George showed me a *luogo (cari luoghi!)* I could not afterwards find it when I wanted it. One of the most worrying parts of these Cretan Travels is the impossibility of chamber pots, and lo! when I went out the door shut to, and I had to roam about to get a priest to open it. It is nearly ten; late hours.

FRIDAY
20 MAY

MONASTERY OF
ARKADHI
AMNATOS
PIGHI
ADHELE
PERIVOLIA
RETHYMNON

Rose before four, having slept very tolerably, thanks to lots of flea powder. Up and dressed 4.50. Coffee: see church — oldish (leave 24 piastres) — then draw on the outside. Ida *would* be lovely, and the whole scene delightful, but clouds stopped all. Then I went up a hill, Gabriel and all the monx too, and drew again, on bits of paper, having put up my large book. Then, at 6.10, we were off. I like Gabriel.

6.30 We have come across, and out of, a very grand ravine, splendidly berocked, beshrubbed and bebirded. The plain is below, and the sea, but foggy and unclear.

7.15 We get to Amnátos: the morning is very hot, close, damp, and the gardens and close olives keep out air. Moslem burying-ground, but no minarets as in Pashley's days.

90

The Monastery of Arkádhi (a painting based on a drawing made on 20 May).

7.45 Rethymnon is seen afar, and the friendly-ugly Akrotíri once more. All we pass is like a great continual garden: corn, *caraba* [carob], olives and fruit trees of many sorts, immensely cultivated and rich.

9 We have just passed Pighí, a very large village utterly hidden in olives. All this territory is amazing for richness.

9.10 We pass through Adhele, another large but concealed village: one is quite surprised by the streets and houses, which are invisible till you are close by them. At a wineshop outside we get some wine. There are the noisiest hens here I ever heard. It seems we are to try to lunch at Perivólia.

10.45 We are actually at Perivólia. The road left the olives after the last town (which like all hereabouts is invisible till one sees it in its streets) and soon descended towards the coast. Konstandís wished to stay at a stream, but as there was no water in it we were obliged to go on, and finally arrived at this place, where after some trouble in getting Konstandís to relinquish staying at a *khan*, we found a nindividual [sic] who allowed us to stay in a plot of walled-in ground — called a garden — over whose walls we hauled the πράγματα [things] and jumped the mule, making the beds and arranging for food below a mulberry tree. The individual, who has to get over a high wall every time he comes (this however happily hides the street and many drunken Turx), has brought us *excellent rakí,* and is gone to get some eggs.

91

Here the dark blue and red girdle costume has gone out, and the semi-Bulgarian worked drab jacket again prevails.

The eggs arrived, and very good they were, which was the first course. Then lettuces plain, and afterwards made into salad by George. Thirdly, μυζήθρα [mizíthra] or *ricotta,* with sugar. We had also perfectly good wine. Therefore, the lunches of Cretan travel are ever to be celebrated. Difficulties exist, not arise, as to our future progress. I reckon 20 hours from here to Halépa — possibly 18 — but that is long work for two days. And hereupon I cannot but think that two or three hours extra work today would be well earned by sleeping at Atsipópoulo, and thus lightening the long morrow. On the other hand, George says, and truly, that tomorrow (being a fast), we shall get nothing to eat at all, and that it is perhaps better to buy mutton and roast it here, staying the night, and starting early tomorrow. I don't know which is best. Always, there is no sunshine today; gray as in England. At the present moment both George and Konstandís are fast asleep (why the muleteer takes off only one boot remains a mystery), and no determination will be come to until they wake.

1 p.m. Calm prevails. 'I see the sea beyond the walls'.

2.30 We 'ave been a-sleeping, and we wake. All is gray, but it is a great comfort to have been as quiet as this in these Perivólia. George and I, by *dolce parole,* convince Konstandís that it is better to go on and sleep at Atsipópoulo, so as not to have to make the *salita* tomorrow. Konstandís says it is a 'good town', so without any recommendation we will try; and thence, by the sea always, endeavour to reach either Neohóri or Arméni, as things may turn out, or some *khan,* which Konstandís says there is.

Kontandís is a wonderfully serene lad, but is taking slowly and gradually to our jokes or chaff, of which his matter-of-fact nature was hitherto innocent.

Konstandís goes off about the mule's shoe, and George remains with me, suffering from an 'undergrowth' of his toe-nails, which I examine and cut, thereby saving the Suliot much pain and trouble. Says George: 'Jesus Christ washed the feet of twelve followers; you may therefore quite rightly cut the nails of one.'

The afternoon is perfectly cloudy and gray, and there was a little thunder: nobody would suppose it to be May — anywhere.

Let us arise and make reddy; it is 3.30.

How ruinous, all ruin, are these places! great fallen stones and small, and lots of plaster: brown okery vestiges (this refers to a little sketch made in notebook). Konstandís returns, 'but with no hope of meat' — or anything else eatable. Good Konstandínos. So we are off at 4.15, utterly cloudy and dull. We pass Rethymnon at five. 'Which do [you] like best?' say I to Konstandís, 'Megalókastro or Rethymnon?' 'Which do I like best; sunshine or darkness, night or day?' says he: «Ποιὸν ἀγαπάω μᾶλλον· ἤ τὸν ἤλιον, ἤ τὴ νύκτα, τὴν ἡμέραν ἤ τὴ σκοτεινή;» Tombstones green and red, and yellow and red. We pass the town and the filthy entrance and the poor afflicted lepers and arrive at the kiosk and water by the sea at 5.30. 'The day is still, the sun is hid'.[83] Atsipópoulo (notes): Setting off at 4.15 we passed outside the walls of

92

Rethymnon at five, and at 5.30 come to the kiosk and well by the sea.

Then came the very stony ascent, a long and tough one, and at 6.15 after floundering latterly in most vilely paved or stoned lanes, we got to the village of Atsipópoulo: a large place, very crooked streets, and the streets at this hour greatly furnished with cattle and other creatures. Asking for the house of the Προεστώς [village president], we arrived there slowly, and the master gladly received us. Entering by a small yard, the lower part of the house was like a Roman *osteria*, a great dark arch spanning it. Hostess agreeable. Children obstreperous. Host very full of words about monasteries, Turx and things in general. 'Friendly' supper: difficult to get through. 'Sleep' to take place in a loft (just over the staircase from the yard),

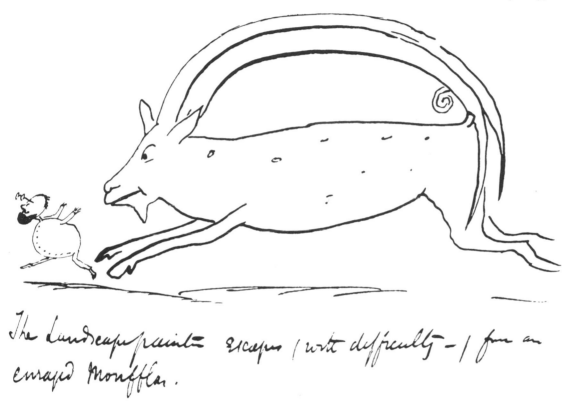

The landscape painter escapes (with difficulty —) from an enraged Moufflar.

mostly full of looms; the yard below containing crowds of sheep and goats. 'These are not the bells I know'[84] but are ceaselessly and terribly disagreeable, as is the stench; and my bed is close to the open staircase. George sleeps beyond two silk looms, and is so far better off than I am: he however does all he can to make me tolerably comfortable before I get into bed.

No sleep all night, from the stench of the stables, over the staircase leading to which my head lay, and from the incessant bleating and bell-ringing, whereby I have a bad headache and am downcast. I have paid Konstandís 25 piastres for the food and two chickens. It is 4.30.

SATURDAY
21 MAY

ATSIPOPOULO

The host last night talked pompously of «λόρδοι ἀπὸ τοὺς Παρισίους κι᾽ ἀπ᾽ ὅλον τὸν κόσμον» ['lordhi from Paris and from all the world'] as frequenting his house. He is like a gigantic Lord Somers.[85]

Out of the town by five. Gray morning.

Tall men — execrable stony road. Trees of every sort of fruity produce. Rejoin main road at the one-arch bridge at 5.30.

6 Down at the little church with the fountain. Tall truculent turbaned travelling Turk joined our party.

At sea-coast road 6.30. At 6.35–6.40 we rest. White Mountains, very lovely. Rocky coast with all the lights and shades of a Cumberland lake.

7.15 Turn the corner of the sea road. 7.40–7.50 Bathe; most lovely cove! Get to the Petrés river at eight: Petrés Kamára.

9 Scrunch always by the sand shore: low corn hills; cloud on higher, above Kourná, and the White Mountains. 9.15 Cross small river. 9.40 Another. 10.20 Leave sea — salt spring — cross low hill. 10.45 Arrive at Armyró.

Noon. We settled below a very thick and high olive. Konstandís was tired, and said, «Ἐρώτησες διατί εἶμαι κουρασμένος, ἐπ᾽ ἐξ ὥρες περπατῶ;» ['You ask me why I'm tired, when I've been walking for six hours?'] Our lunch was two small cold chickens (I could have eaten six or eight such), bread and cheese and Kissamos wine, and we were happy enough. The loud waterfall is a delight; also the bee-eater's whistling cry, the green and the sunshine. At one I am awakened by George, who is wandering about. Say I: 'Do you ever talk of these travels to Tatiané?'[86] 'They think it all one the same as from Kastrádhes to Corfu — so I say no more.' The oleanders are lovely, but it is not a healthful spot. Konstandís says there is a good *khan* three hours off, near Neohóri, so I shall go there.

1.20 George suddenly appears with two huge bunches of green, which turn out to be watercresses. At 1.30 Konstandís rebels, and says he will go, and we all move off, at 1.45. 2–2.15 We do not cross the river: very pleasing leafy scenes. But I don't like being forced to go by a double-tongued[87] muleteer before the hour I and he had arranged, so I am cross. The path leads along a valley, low hills on each side, and the lower (green) spurs of the Sphakiot mountains on the left. At 3.15, having coasted the river, we cross it. 4.30 Woody gully ever. A fountain. 4.45 Apokórona. 5.50 Pass river. *Khan*. Scenery. The last day of my Cretan travels, I suppose: a fatiguing day. Six hours before lunch, and four afterwards, but what choice is there? The early part of the morning break-leg and sprain-ankle work: then the wearying toil over the rocks to the Kamára bridge. A respite by a bathe, and crossing the river, and the beauty of vast flox of goats on the sand; the blue bay of Armyró beyond and the snow range above. Then the tedious and fatiguing nine miles of sand till at eleven there was rest below an olive at Armyró. Sleep, ill-broken by anger, and I walked alone through the close muffy valley till I had reached Apokórona. But at 5.30, when I asked George where was the *khan*, he said we had passed it half an hour, and he had said nothing because I had declared I would go to Arméni, which, though disagreeable, was true. So we went

Apokórona, 5.30. p.m., 21 May.

on, but soon, finding another *khan* was near, I said, «"Ας πᾶμε ἐκεῖ — *etchí*»[88] ['let's go there']: and so we have settled there, albeit it be a beastly futile hole. From the river a lovely scene is beheld, and I half think the river scenes of Crete are its best claim to beauty for paintings. At the *khan* George gave me water, and is as attentive as if he had not walked ten hours; and he did what he could to soften me to the muleteer.

    9.30 Dear me! we are a family party of four, besides a cove who has come in to make a hubblebubble. So, retiring to this nasty place, I found George setting to work, as if he had been sitting still all day, boiling a fowl and rice; and after a while I, he and Konstandís make an excellent supper on it. Rice soup, a boiled fowl, respectable wine and *café*. We have since got parked for the night — if only that smoking man had not come in. Crickets abound. Even yet, I hate the thought of giving up Sphakiá, for Askýphou is only four hours off!

95

Our mule.
(Konstandís Manosákis.)
8 a.m.?, 22 May.

<table>
<tr><td>SUNDAY
22 MAY

APOKORONA
HALEPA</td><td>We are up and ready at 4.30, but someone has stolen the φόρτομα [baggage] cord, and there is nothing to tie on the things with: a horrid bore, as Konstandís is obliged to go up to the village to try to get another. We start at 5.30. The valley and mountains are magnificent, and I draw till 5.45.

7.30 We are at the top of the Palaiókastro ascent, looking down on Akrotíri and Suda. I regret not having made better Apokórona drawings.

8 At the fount and fig tree, on the descent. Oleanders in bloom!</td></tr>
</table>

MONDAY
23 MAY

HALEPA
HANIA

Rose at six, and rewrote journal and letters to T. Cooper and John Day[89] till eight. Went to the town with George and called on Guarracino. Drew £20 through him on Drummond's and also £20 through Mr Drummond Hay on Drummond's (the latter for him to repay Kalokairinós of Herákleion). Called on the Pasha, who was very polite, and saw Henry Moazza, who gave me some names for Phré and Sphakiá, to which I resolve on going, though the kind Hays would rather keep me here. They are the very kindest people I have known many a long day. Left good George to buy various things and walked back to Halépa alone. Dinner — always pleasant. Later, after singing and playing, went with Drummond Hay to Mr Dendrino's and returned at six. Arranged things for tomorrow; George and I are to go in the simplest modes of ancient or modern travel. Newspapers, tea and cold meat, and playing and singing till 9.30. Bed. I hate leaving these kind people.

TUESDAY
24 MAY

I and George were ready before four, and off from the kind Hays by 4.30. I took with a hair-, nail- and tooth-brush, sponge, soap, quinine, pencils, two pairs of sox, a light cloak and a handkerchief. Also a piece of Stilton cheese (the maggots in which so

96

Suda Bay, 5 a.m., 24 May.

scandalized Hassan Eyn), and a flask of wine. George carried my heavy folio, two loaves of bread and a great piece of mutton — all these eatables and drinkables being only about a third of what the good Hays had wished us to take. Down we went, and by sunrise I was drawing Suda Bay, which with the hills and Ida (perverse mountain!) were like pure glass. Then followed the long ascent, easier in the cool of the morning, and then the go down, towards the valley. I drew three times, each time delighting more in the beautiful scene, the great charm of which is the contrast between the dark full green of the olive, and the lilac hills and the broad pure snow above. All the great and lovely characteristics of Cretan landscape are expressed in that valley plain of Apokórona. When we came down into the valley or plain, and reached the water gushing out everywhere, about 9 or 9.30, we resolved to stay here, and so, having first tried a plane tree and failed, we finally fixes below an olive, whence we look on the green bright quiet world: the rivery rills sparkling at our feet, and the bright snow beyond; birds singing everywhere, but no nightingales. Greenery is the nature of Crete: green — green — green and good! George has fetched some

97

The plain of Apokórona, 8 a.m., 24 May.

more wine from the *khan,* and a pitcher of cold water, and now for Stilton cheese. Shall we get to Phré, or Askýphou today? A funny voyage this! and takeable with no-one but George Kokáli. Geese, white, abound below in the green. We linger, and it is now 11.30 by their account, for I have no watch. Three or four men as usual come around: one, an intelligent fellow. The universal suavity of these Cretans is certainly wonderful. They say, sleeping here after May or June is not good. Everybody round talks, but I would gladly sleep as George does. We set off about one. The water and green are a delight. Soon we lose our way, missing the road to the river; but it is no matter, since the valley is straight before us. Olive groves. A sleeping man with wandering mules and baggage speak of security. Birds warble and twitter endless. I drew Palaiókastro, and then we went on, endeavouring to keep the way to the *khan* below Neohóri, but somehow we got wrong, and came up close under Mahairí. Thence, by closest and stuffiest stony lanes, we worked up to Neohóri, Païdhohóri and eventually Pemónia; and now, four or five, we are not very far off Phré. But the way has been utterly uninteresting, both as to distant views and near foreground, one village being like all, and olives and close trees round all. Closely wrapped-up boxed

98

On the road to Phré, 11.30 a.m., 24 May.

cottages, olives, figs, etc. etc.; I would have gone back twenty times if possible. Arriving at Phré, a man volunteered to show us the house of Manouél Tzoustákis, and entering the large village (of course it was full of ruined — except indeed four or five churches: Aghios Gheórghios, Aghia Triádha, Aghia Panaghía, and a huge new one — buildings). Mr Tzoustákis's house was not very inviting to see (he himself a plain worthy sort of man), neither out nor in, but he was polite and hearty and gave me coffee. I decided I would try and see what there might be out of doors, so went with George and the new volunteer guide, Nikoláki, which latter took me to a point at some distance, whence the view of Ida is by far the best I have yet seen, and truly fine. Never till now have I had much respect for Ida. A dream-like vast pile of pale pink and lilac, with endless gradations and widths of distance, and the long curve of sand from Rethymnon hills to Armyró. So I drew till long after sunset, and then came to this place, where I washed in a cheese plate and sat down with what patience I could. Supper was as usual brought on a table, with filthy napkins (Nikoláki being invited by host), good rice soup and boiled fowl, *kolokýthia* [vegetable marrows] and *alici* [anchovies] (very nasty) and amazing wine. Painfully conventional health-drinking,

99

Psilorítis (Mount Ida) from Phré, 7 p.m., 24 May.

but the host is an intelligent man, and Nikoláki has travelled in Egypt. But the vermin prevented any rest of body or mind. At nine I put my cloak on the odious bed and lay down, not to sleep but to bear agonies of vermin bites. George on a distant divan at one end; the snory groany host at the other. Fleas are too awful to describe. *Misery*.

WEDNESDAY
25 MAY

PHRE
BABALI-HANI
HALEPA

No sleep all night long, and extreme misery. Resolved therefore finally to go back, the more that I have now one really good view of Mount Ida, and of the valley of Apokórona; and as I perceive the nature of the Sphakian mountains would preclude much possibility of picturesqueness. So I rose from my detestable couch, and again drew Ida from the housetop, and I bought two Sphakian carpets for 500 piastres. At 5.30 we set off downwards, Nikoláki carrying the *roba*. We came down to the Babalí-Hani, of which we had heard good reports, but lo! as George predicted, there was not even a glass of *rakí!* Here we joined the road from Rethymnon, and I went on to the *khan* we had slept at below Neohóri, drawing before I crossed the river; low down, as well as from an upper *khan*. The colour of these scenes is truly lovely, and the

100

Psilorítis (Mount Ida) from Phré, before sunrise, 4.30 a.m., 25 May.

rock of Mahairí splendid. Thence, at 8.30, we got to our *khan* of yesterday, and the detached olive tree, where we made lunch the last, on wondrous mutton, chicken, herring, bread and cheese and wine, with water from the many-headed springs at our feet. Somewhen about eleven we started (I drawing once more by the way), and began our *salita*, resting on the way about noon. All the Sphakian mountains are clouded: Q.E.D. Perseverance enabled us to conquer the long ascent, and now I suppose it is 1 p.m., and we are resting at the fig tree fount on our way down the Gulf of Suda. A hot long walk brought us to Halépa about 2.30, or three, and glad indeed was I to be once more at the Consul's house. Both the Hays received us as usual, and one seems to have lived here all one's life. After a tub and wash, George (cook being out) made a good pilaf, which with cold beef and salad and wine was princely. Afterwards the Hays walked out, and I read and fell asleep, waking to find little Madeleine lying by me with her arms round my neck kissing me and patting my eyes. Darling little child. I was awfully sleepy, and tea hardly revived me, so before nine I went to bed, and slept instantaneously totally. What a blessing is this family!

THURSDAY 26 MAY HALEPA	Did not rise before six, having slept amazingly. Made two designs from the Mount Ida and Apokórona drawings of yesterday and Tuesday. The sky is cloudy and all is misty. At twelve, papers. Archer Clive has got a First Class, which delights me.[90] Cholmondeley's eldest brother, Owen of Condover, is dead.[91] Dinner at one, always pleasant: asking for more meat, little Madeleine said 'More!' ' "Yes if you please" you should say', said her father. 'Yes if you please, kind Sir, she said, Sir, she said', said the funny little girl. After dinner, Mrs Hay being away, I offered to go to Mrs Hay Senior and divulge the marriage: but he said he must do it himself. Played and sang to the little girls (a little Maltese comes to play with Madeleine) till 3.30, when we went down to the town, the Hays leaving me at the Arab tents, where I drew: afterwards I went into the hateful town and sketched on the port, and bought some toys for little Madeleine, and George and I returned by six. The evening is quite foggy and overcast. Tea and cold beef, neither of which are good for me: singing afterwards till ten. Bed.
FRIDAY 27 MAY HALEPA	Rose before six. Made ten numeral drawings for Madeleine and worked at my two Cretan designs in colour and wrote my journal. But I took medicine and got horridly irritable. Slept again and at one, dinner. After which, at three or four, went with George to the Suda road and drew the hills and plain. The blacks and Arabs were having a fête: all the sky was gray and cloudy *qua* rainy. Evening: tea and music. It certainly is vexatious not to have seen Selino or Sphakiá, but it was *not* possible, and it is of no use to regret the impossible. Sphakiá must be ranked with Istamboul, Castro Giovanni, Nazareth, Broussa and other unattained places.
SATURDAY 28 MAY HALEPA	Slept very ill, along of tea drinking. Rose at seven. Bought another carpet, 180 piastres. Wrote out lots of Tennyson for Hay, and made ten more drawings for Madeleine and wrote up journal to the 13th. Dinner at one, cheerful happy, and afterwards Mr Hay and Madeleine were both vaccinated. She is a darling little child. Went with George at 3.45 to a field among olives and drew the city: but it has been perfectly hazy all day long. Nevertheless, there is a pearly grace of colour ever about this view. At tea, I had wine and water instead of tea, and sang afterward till nearly ten. Verily, this house is a blessing. Great wind at night.
SUNDAY 29 MAY HALEPA	Very lovely and fresh. This early morning life is the beauty of luxury in these southern places; and the quiet and brightness and cleanliness of this lovely house is a blessing. Rose at 5.30 and wrote out journal, up to the 15th, till noon or later, making ten more drawings for the little girl also. Just as I was 'changing myself' Hay brought in Dendrino to 'visit' me, whereat I was decomposed. Dinner at one. It is now four and I have been finishing Madeleine's number-pictures. Slept and read till six, when I walked in the garden and also gave the monkey some onions. Then, with Mr and Mrs Hay, walked out to the Arab huts and beyond. The sea air was delicious, but I have

Haniá, 5.30–6 p.m., 28 May.

never seen any sunset here warmer in colour than those of Hastings: a sort of pearly silver mist involves all the isle. But the Sphakian mountains, though now almost snowless, are very grand; and so are the Riza hills, and the plain, and we shall not see many places lovelier. Came back. At eight, tea-supper, and afterwards sang them sixteen Tennyson songs. So to bed at ten.

Rose at five and finished packing. Morning less windy, but with clouds. Verily this place is most lovely. Wrote to Drummond's and to T. Cooper. At ten, George, having procured two asses, took all the luggage — nine pieces to wit — into the city. My bed, George's bed (2), two saddlebags, drawings, George's bags, black bag, hatbox = 9. I gave 40 piastres each to Andréa cook, Hassan Eyn, Kavass and Agnese, and 20 to groom.

MONDAY
30 MAY

HALEPA
HANIA

At 4 p.m. left the kind Hays with sorrow, as did George, and came to the detestable streets of Haniá. Went to the Consulate, and thence to the Pasha to leave a P.P.C., but His Excellency saw George and begged I would walk upstairs, so I did, and sat two minutes, with a succeeding affectionate and cordial 'addío'. Thence to

Guarracino's house, but only Peter and David the dog were there. Back to Consulate, where I changed money and paid 376½ piastres for places, giving tips to kavasses etc. etc. After this, good-natured Henry Moazza called, and later Boone; and then, as no steamer came, I went to sleep on a sofa.

Haniá, from the *Persia*, 4 a.m., 31 May.

The steamer came at 2 a.m. and it is now 3.30 and nearly daylight. Confusions, etc. etc. Went on board the old *Persia*, but before I did so the postman, at the very last moment, gave me a letter from Franklin Lushington, sent to *Candia*! and so gone wrong and delayed. Also, Kavass Zeriff, having been sent to Candia by the Pasha, and returning by this boat, came up just in time to say goodbye to me, and for me to tell him I had left a *baksheesh* for him at the Consul's. Meanwhile it is 6.30, and the *Persia* is off. 6.45 All Crete diminishes, fades, vanishes; but we see Ghoniá, we see Plataniá, we see the pleasant Halépa, where we have spent so many happy days. We see the long range of Sphakian mountains, now nearly snowless. Last of all, lo! Ida fades. «Ποιός εἶναι αὐτός;» ['Who's that?'] I hear numbers saying, and «Εἶναι λόρδος τους.» ['It's their *lordhos*.'] 2 p.m. The day is one of those only known in southern worlds, and were it not for the disgusting community around, nothing could be more delightful. The way in which these mongrel filths of the third class insist on occupying all the best places! Slept from nine to ten and then breakfasted, with the little second Captain and the third, and a German or Italo-German. Since, I have been sitting on deck, watching Milos and Antímilos and other forthcoming isles. The Captain seems to think the Marseilles boat goes on Saturday; short span for me! George must go by

104

Greece. I hate his leaving me. Read (*Lutfullah's Life*),[92] and slept till three and sat in the saloon till four, because the second class take all the room on deck. Dinner, and now at 6.30 Syra is in sight, or rather, near. The multitude of 'Isles of Greece' is quite uncommon and lovely, but the filth and crowd of the deck prevents my staying there, except to point out various isles to George. Later, just before sunset, the deck was clearer and I sat there. It is curious to remember how little colour there was in the Crete sunsets compared with those here: yellow, red, green, such as I see now, there I never saw: but always a pearly warm gray. About eight we reached Syra. A wonderful voyage!

There was a young person of Crete
Whose toilet was far from complete . . .

NOTES

1 Spiro Kokáli, brother of Lear's servant George.

2 Lear's doctor is suggesting that the Jews were happier under British rule. Although the Greek Constitution guaranteed freedom of religion, there was considerable anti-semitic feeling in Greece which especially manifested itself at Easter when the burning of Judas in effigy sometimes got out of hand. In 1864 the Sephardic community in Corfu numbered about 5,000. Although they were apprehensive about the change of government, few in fact left the island until the pogrom of 1891.

3 'alas! indeed yes! (12 August 1865) yesterday H. De Vere was killed.' (Lear's note.) After leaving Corfu, Francis Horatio De Vere, a major in the Royal Engineers, became an instructor at Brompton Barracks, Chatham. He was shot on 11 August 1865, apparently by a sapper who bore him a grudge, and died on 22 August. Lear was fond of his little girl Mary, and used to make illustrated alphabets for her.

4 'Meanwhile Captⁿ. Deverills ganders 2 eldest wives have brought out a brood of 10 lovely green puffy fluffy goslings, — & my whole pleasure in life is to watch them.' (Lear to Chichester Fortescue, 31 March 1864.)

5 Evelyn Baring (later Lord Cromer) had been acting as aide to Sir Henry Storks, the Lord High Commissioner of the Ionian Islands. Lear already knew his cousin Thomas George Baring (Lord Northbrook); it was at his house in 1867 that he started to prepare the Cretan journal for publication.

6 An earlier, Levantine, version of 'The Cummerbund' (*Laughable Lyrics*, 1877). *Bulbul*: a middle-eastern bird, a member of the thrush family; one of the characters in Thackeray's *Our Street* is called Clarence Bulbul.

7 The British Ambassador.

8 The Revd Dr John Hill and his wife had been sent to Athens by the American Episcopal Church in 1830. There they founded the American School for Girls, a charitable institution which trained generations of Greek schoolteachers. Lear had previously visited the Hills in 1848. The Hill School still continues today.

9 Count Sponnek was a Danish politician and economist at the court of the new King George I of the Hellenes, the younger son of the King of Denmark. The nineteen-year-old king had come to the throne the previous October — Lear thought of applying for the position so that he could be 'King Lear' — and it was as a settlement of his accession that England had ceded Corfu and the other Ionian Islands to Greece. George succeeded the Bavarian King Otho, the first king of liberated Greece, whose deposition in 1862 had been little regretted. Just as Otho had surrounded himself with Bavarian advisers, so King George relied on Danes, but he proved himself more flexible and prepared to accept the dictates of the Greek government than his predecessor.

10 Lear's companion on his travels in Boeotia and Euboea in 1848 had been Charles Church, nephew of the famous veteran of the Greek War of Independence, Sir Richard Church. Sir Richard (1784–1873) came from a Quaker family and ran away from home as a boy to enlist in the Napoleonic Wars. A distinguished career in the British army was followed by an invitation to command the Greek forces in the War of Independence. After the war, Church made his home in Athens and continued to play an influential role in Greek politics. In 1864 he can only have been 79 or 80 — not, as Lear thought, 82.

11 No Englishman of note would have visited Athens without a letter of introduction to George Finlay, author of the monumental *History of Greece from its conquest by the Romans to the*

present time, B.C. 146 to A.D. 1864, 7 vols. (Oxford, 1877). Finlay (1799–1875) had travelled with Byron during the Greek War of Independence and energetically promoted the Greek cause. Afterwards he stayed on in Athens, hoping to set an example by investing in land, but ultimately becoming embroiled in lawsuits (one against King Otho himself) and embittered by the inefficiencies of Greek agriculture. Finlay loved Greece and was an outspoken critic of what he saw as her political and social shortcomings. When Lear visited him he was just about to embark as *The Times* correspondent in Athens (1864–74) on what was to become a famous series of newspaper articles.

12 Lear disliked the 'Tory-furious' and 'somewhat muzzy' P. F. Campbell Johnston whom he had met in Corfu. Johnston continued to dog Lear's footsteps, even trying to borrow the manuscript of his Cretan journal (diary, 18 August 1867).

13 Thomas Cooper and his wife kept house for Lear in his London lodgings at 15 Stratford Place.

14 Edgar Drummond, of Drummond & Co., was Lear's banker. Mrs Mildmay had bought a watercolour of Athens and Captain Lawson two oils, one of Parga and one of Ochrid.

15 Lear's sister Eleanor (Ellen) Newsom (1800–1885) to whom he wrote regularly. She married a director of the Bank of England and lived in Leatherhead, where Lear visited. After her death Lear wrote: 'We had but little in common intellectually, yet never disagreed at all. Spite of her narrow Calvinistic theories, she was absolutely good and charitable in practice . . .' (*Later Letters*, p. 303).

16 An old friend and lifelong correspondent of Lear's.

17 Elizabeth Nevill, mother of Lear's boyhood friend William Nevill. She died on 18 March.

18 By 'Museum' Lear means the hill of the Mouseion, on the summit of which is the Roman monument of Philopappus. The 'Lantern of Demosthenes' is the Choregic Monument of Lysicrates below the southeast corner of the Acropolis. According to Murray, 'the resemblance of the edifice to the large Turkish hand-lanterns easily explains its name.'

19 Constantin Athanasio's shop in Hermes Street was the best known shop in Athens for photographs of tourist sights.

20 As British Consul at Thessalonica he had helped Lear escape a cholera outbreak in 1848. He later became Consul at Smyrna, where he died on 3 March 1864.

21 Franklin Lushington, a lawyer and classical scholar, had toured Greece with Lear in 1849; their friendship, though never as close and reliable as Lear would have liked, was nonetheless life-long. Lushington helped Lear prepare some of his work for publication and, as his legatee and executor, was also responsible for destroying some of his papers after his death.

22 The main town of Syra was divided into the Catholic upper town, founded by the Venetians in the thirteenth century, and the newer port of Hermoúpolis, established by Greek refugees from the islands of Chios and Psará in 1822.

23 The miraculous cures ascribed to the icon of the Panaghía Tiniótissa (Virgin of Tinos) make the island of Tinos as famous to Greek Orthodox as Lourdes is to Roman Catholics. Thousands of pilgrims, including the old and sick, converge on Tinos from all over Greece for the feast days of the Annunciation and the Dormition of the Virgin when the icon is taken out of its shrine and carried round the town. The pilgrims Lear saw were returning from the feast of the Annunciation on 25 March; 6 April in the English calendar.

24 Frank Ringler Drummond Hay, British Consul in Crete May 1863 to January 1865.

25 Elizabeth Kontaxákis, notorious in Levantine circles as an independent-minded bluestocking. She had been educated at the Hills' school in Athens. 'Her profound scholarship, wit, enthusiasm and energy are characteristics of the rarest kind among the Greek women of the present day, and have therefore given her a wide celebrity. Of course, her position is not

entirely a pleasant one. While some of the Greeks are justly proud of her, others dislike and some fear her. Her will, talent and a certain diplomatic aptness give her considerable power and influence, the possession of which always excites jealousy and enmity in a Greek community. Consequently, she has many enemies, and is assailed at times by the meanest slanders and intrigues. She is about thirty years of age, of a medium stature, and, with the exception of her lambent black eyes, there is nothing very striking in her appearance. She speaks English, Greek and French with almost equal fluency, and has the ancient Greek authors at her fingers' ends. She talks with great rapidity, ease, and with a rare clearness and sequence of ideas, in narration. I was interested at finding in her the same quickness and acuteness of mental perception for which the old Greeks were famous.' (Bayard Taylor, *Travels*, New York, 1880, v, p. 93.)

26 Paramythiótti had been Lear's landlord in Corfu and had given him a letter of introduction to Mr Dendrino, the Russian Consul-General in Crete.

27 Supreme Judge of the Ionian Islands.

28 President of the Ionian Assembly.

29 The large cobbles of the roads themselves, rather than the footpath which the modern sense of the word suggests: '. . . evil awaits the man who tries to walk with nailed boots on the rounded, slippery stones of a Turkish pavement!' (*Journals of a Landscape Painter in Albania*, p. 23.)

30 A village in Corfu; the name means 'Ascension'. Lear thought it 'one of the loveliest spots on earth'.

31 Although he had no formal musical training, Lear loved to compose settings of his favourite poems. He frequently moved himself and his audience to tears when he performed his compositions — sometimes to tears of laughter as he sang nonsense versions of the poems he usually took so seriously. Mrs Hay obviously shared his sense of humour: one evening at Halépa they amused themselves translating Tennyson's 'As through the land at eve we went' into literal Italian, so that the line 'We fell out, my wife and I' became 'Siamo cascati fuori, — io ed anche la mia moglie' (letter to Emily Tennyson, 31 July 1864). On 29 May (see p. 103) Lear sang as many as sixteen of his Tennyson settings — all but two of the eighteen he had composed by that date. In addition to 'As through the land', the Hays would have heard such favourites of Lear's as 'Sweet and low', 'Tears, idle tears', 'Come not, when I am dead' and 'Break, break, break'.

32 The inhabitants of the southern province of Sphakiá were a law unto themselves during the period of Turkish rule. Their inaccessible situation and fierce reputation had won them a measure of *de facto* autonomy and the Pasha would be reluctant to have them hob-nobbing with foreigners.

33 Lear visited Hastings several times; perhaps he is remembering the summer of 1852, when he stayed at Clive Vale Farm with Holman Hunt. The Plymouth memories are probably those of his first visit to Devon and Cornwall, in the summer of 1837.

34 Partner in the firm of Collas & Michel, 'Administration générale des Phares de l'Empire Ottoman'.

35 '. . . saw a goat killed — & an attempt at Mule making — a Gentleman & 10 men ass-isting' (Lear's diary, Samos, Cephalonia, 2 May 1863).

36 An ironic reference to the 'dreaming spires' of Matthew Arnold's Oxford?

37 What provoked this outburst? It appears on the diary page for 20 April, separated by a line from the rest of the day's notes. Lear also includes it in the journal entry for 20 April although it would seem to follow more naturally after the following day's encounter with the monks of the Akrotíri. Monasticism tended to set Lear off — see his famous comments on Mount Athos, *Letters*, pp. 38–42: '. . . these muttering, miserable, mutton-hating,

man-avoiding, misogynic, morose, and merriment-marring, monotoning, many-mule-making, mocking, mournful, minced-fish and marmalade masticating Monx. Poor old pigs!' He was interested in the religious controversies of his day, reading Froude, Newman, Renan and Colenso, and often comments on discussions and sermons he has heard. He was liberal in outlook, a church-goer though a non-communicant, and hated bigotry and sectarianism. He particularly objected to the Athanasian Creed, and generally sympathized with the Broad Churchmen, here Benjamin Jowett (1817–1893), Rowland Williams (1817–1870) and his old friend Arthur Penrhyn Stanley (1815–1881) of whom he wrote, 'I have a kind of mixed affection and interest and admiration for him I never felt united for anybody.' His attack is reserved for the hardliners: George Anthony Denison (1805–1896), the acrimonious Old High Churchman, and for Paul Cullen (1803–1878), Archbishop of Dublin, and John Cumming (1807–1881) of the National Scottish Church, author of *The Romish Church a Dumb Church* — 'two nasty yet approximate extremes' in Lear's opinion. He once suggested sending a copy of his *Book of Nonsense* to Archbishop Cullen.

38 A favourite quotation of Lear's: he wrote of his Italian muleteer that 'he was, as King Charles the Second is said to have said of somebody [Sidney Godolphin], "never *in*, nor ever *out* of, the way" ' (*Southern Calabria and the Kingdom of Naples*, p. 79).

39 Eliza Duckworth, a friend and regular customer of Lear's, died on 29 March.

40 Western travellers believed that only icons were allowed in Orthodox churches and Pashley (I, p. 19) was surprised to see the iron crucifix of Aghios Elevthérios, to which miraculous powers were ascribed. Henry Fanshawe Tozer (*The Islands of the Aegean*, Oxford, 1890, p. 37) thought the crucifix unusual enough to be worth sketching (see illustration on p. 40).

41 Lear's closest friend. He had met Fortescue (1823–1898) as a young man in Rome in 1845 and they went on meeting and corresponding on easy good terms for the rest of their lives. Lear followed Fortescue's career as a Liberal politician with interest and affection as he was appointed Privy Councillor (1864 — see p. 41), Secretary of State for Ireland (1865), President of the Board of Trade (1871) and President of the Council (1883). When Fortescue became Lord Privy Seal (1881) Lear invented a series of adventures for the 'Phoca' (seal) or 'Phoca Privata' — 'that dear old beast': 'I wonder how you get the creature to Balmoral, for it cannot live so many hours without water . . . I imagine therefore that you take him either in an indiarubber bag or a tub-box . . .' (*Later Letters*, p. 266).

42 The plane trees, after which the village of Plat}aniá was named: 'Vines twine around most of these platanes, and are of a size unknown in France or Italy, the thickness of many of their stems being that of an ordinary man's waist . . . The varied scenery produced by these noble plane-trees, in the valley of Plataniá, is very beautiful, and is one of the objects best worth viewing by those who visit Khaniá, and can stay only a short time in the island.' (Pashley, II, p. 22.)

43 Tennyson, 'The Lotos-Eaters'.

44 The artist who travelled with Pashley and drew most of the illustrations for his book.

45 Some fine seventeenth-century icons, still on view today, which had been sent away for safe keeping during the 1821–27 War of Independence: 'The church of this monastery contains a greater number of those paintings with which the Greeks love to adorn the interior of their places of religious worship, than is usually met with in Crete. They were all sent to Trieste at the outbreaking of the revolution, and thus escaped destruction.' (Pashley, II, p. 28.)

46 Tennyson, *Maud*, 1, IX.

47 Bernard Husey Hunt, a friend of Lear's since the 1820s.

48 Storax *(Styrax officinalis)*.

49 Any ancient site tended to be *kastro* to the local people. Lear is here visiting the acropolis of Polyrrhenia, where archaic and classical remains are overlaid by Roman, Frankish and Turkish masonry.

50 H. S. Ongley, Consul in Crete 1837–58; later Consul at Patras.

51 Like Lear's Old Man, threatened by a cow: 'I will sit on this stile, and continue to smile, / Which may soften the heart of that Cow.' (*A Book of Nonsense*, 1846.)

52 The Venetian fort of Kastélli-Kissámou, built in 1550 and incorporating much material from the ancient Kissamos.

53 The bells that bothered Lear in the early hours of Saturday morning were summoning the villagers to the Easter week service of the Epitáphios which commemorates the burial of Christ. The Epitáphios, a symbolic representation of Christ's tomb, is profusely decorated with flowers and placed in the centre of the church. Towards the end of the long service, it is carried around the outside of the church, or round the main streets of the village, and all follow, as at a funeral, with lighted candles. (In Greece today, this service is held on the evening of Good Friday.) Later on in the day the villagers reassemble in the church for further services, culminating in the midnight resurrection service. At the proclamation 'Christ is risen!' fireworks are let off, pistols shot, and bells rung. After the service, people return to their houses for their first meat meal following the great Lenten fast and for the first cracking of the traditional red eggs. The celebrations continue throughout the whole of Easter Sunday when Greeks keep open house and there is much feasting, drinking and merry-making.

54 Tennyson, *Maud*, 2, I.

55 Tennyson, 'Come not, when I am dead'; Lear had published a musical setting of this poem in 1859 (see also note 31).

56 The Brussels episodes in *Villette* offer several parallels with Lear's life in Corfu. He must have sympathized with Charlotte Brontë's plain but passionate heroine Lucy Snowe, with her sad childhood, her isolation and emotional breakdown in a foreign town and her ambivalent attitudes to love and marriage.

57 *Rakí* (also called *tsikoudhiá* in Crete) is the colourless spirit distilled twice over from the grape skins and stalks left in the wine press after the grapes have been pressed. It is widely drunk in Crete as an aperitif and is traditionally offered to guests on arrival, with a sweet and a glass of water. Each monastery would have had its own still.

58 On his trip to the Near East in 1862 the Prince of Wales ('Bertie', the future King Edward VII) was accompanied by his tutor the Hon. Robert Bruce, and by Lear's friend A. P. Stanley who acted as guide and chaplain. Bruce fell ill in Palestine and later died in Athens, where he had been left behind to recover. The Prince and Bruce had visited Lear's Rome studio in 1859.

59 English or Turkey oaks (*Quercus robur* or *Quercus cerris*) rather than valonia oaks (*Quercus ægilops* or *Quercus vallonea*). In his drawings Lear also distinguishes the Greek πρινάρι, kermes oak (*Quercus coccifera*).

60 George Kalokairinós was Consular Agent in Rethymnon until 1867 when his son-in-law Harálambos Petihákis (see p. 63) took over.

61 One of the main exports of Rethymnon, according to Spratt.

62 Lear must have stopped to draw on the way; on the sketch of the Rethymnon shore-line dated 8 May, 11 a.m., he has written 'Break, break, break'.

63 Lear is confusing two different herbs. Ἀλάδανο or ladanum is the dark brown resin, used in perfumery, which is collected from *Cistus villosus creticus;* dittany, used in perfumes and

liqueurs, is *Origanum dictamnus.*

64 Lear had never really liked Gould, author of the bird books, for whom he first worked as illustrator in 1831: '[Gould] is always a hog', he wrote in his diary (27 November 1863) and 'a more singularly offensive mannered man than G. hardly can be!' (9 November 1863.)

65 The Farquhar family were old friends of Lear's.

66 This was George Kalokairinós's brother, Lysimachus, Vice-Consul in Herákleion. There was also another brother, Minos, the amateur archaeologist who, in 1878, was the first to dig on the site of Knossos: '. . . [part of the palace] had been the scene of a promiscuous dig in search of ancient objects at the hands of a native explorer . . . Mr Minos Kalokairinos, a merchant of Candia, much interested in Cretan antiquities.' (Arthur Evans, *The Palace of Minos,* 1921–36, IV, p. 621.)

67 After playing an energetic role in the Cretan uprisings of 1821–27, 1841 and 1858, Korakas was appointed local inspector of the χωροφυλακή (gendarmerie) by the Turkish author-ities. When Lear met him he was enjoying a short spell as a private citizen before commanding 20,000 insurgents in 1866. His house in Pobia was burned by Turkish irregulars and in reprisal he set fire to dozens of Turkish villages. He died, much decorated, in 1889 at the age of 87.

68 Bugs; 'F sharps' = fleas.

69 In Cretan pronounciation, Greek 'k' (κ) and 'h' (χ) are softened to 'tch' and 'sh'. Hence 'metosshi' for *metóhi,* and also 'etchi' for *ekí* (p. 95).

70 The large number of British aristocrats among early travellers in the Levant gave the Greek language the word *lordhos* for any foreigner in European dress. The usage survived into the twentieth century.

71 The cultivation of silk cocoons was still a flourishing cottage industry in Crete, though it was soon to be threatened by the opening-up of European trade with China and Japan. The larvae were kept indoors and fed on mulberry leaves. Lear had come across silkworms before and found them disagreeable: '. . . so completely did silkworms seem the life and air, end and material, of all Staíti, that we felt more than half sure, on contemplating three or four suspicious-looking dishes, that those interesting lepidoptera formed a great part of the groundwork of our banquet — silkworms plain boiled, stewed chrysalis, and moth tarts.' (*Southern Calabria and the Kingdom of Naples,* pp. 53–54.)

72 The Sussex village of Peppering, near his sister Sarah's house, where Lear had enjoyed the company of the Drewitt family from the 1820s onwards. As so often happened, the words of Tennyson's 'Break, break, break' come into his mind.

73 An island off Corfu; fortifications were built all over it by the French in 1798 and dismantled by the British in 1864.

74 Lear had set Shelley's 'Lament' ('O world! O life! O time!') to music.

75 Sir Stratford and Lady Canning (later Lord and Lady Stratford de Redcliffe) were old friends of Lear's; they had looked after him at the British Embassy when he arrived in Constantinople ill in 1848, and he had also met them in Italy and Corfu.

76 Lear had first met Williams (1800–1885) in Rome in 1837, and kept in touch with him until his death. In September 1884 he wrote to Henry Bruce: 'To me, P. W.'s colour was always truthful & lovely, & his delineations of Scenery on the Roman Campagna & in the neighbouring mountains absolutely perfect, & I owe him much for his having introduced me to such places as Civitella, Olevana, etc., — as well as to my constant observation of his work.'

77 James Duffield Harding (1798–1863), author of *The Tourist in Italy,* studied with Prout and is one of Lear's links with the eighteenth-century tradition of landscape painting. It is not clear that Lear was ever a pupil of Harding's but he here acknowledges his influence *via*

Daniel Fowler (1810–1894) who trained in Harding's studio between 1831 and 1834 and first met Lear in about 1832. The two worked together and Lear gave Fowler several sketches in the rather gloomy Harding manner, some signed 'by Lear after Harding'. Robert Leake Gale was Fowler's brother-in-law and accompanied him on his Italian journey of 1834–35.

78 'N.B. interpolated sentence, cause unknown' (Lear's note, 30 May 1864). *The Record*: an evangelical newspaper.

79 The 'columns, friezes, etc. etc.' were from Gortyn: '. . . columns, statues, fragments of all kinds have been absorbed in constructing and patching up modern Ayii Dheka. If you go about it properly, you can usually get some of the local people to show choice pieces, built into courtyards, stairways and houses.' (John Bowman, *The Travellers' Guide to Crete*, 1972, p. 174.)

80 Tennyson, 'Œnone'.

81 Unidentified.

82 Another Mrs Hay: not Mrs Drummond Hay of Halépa, but Kalítza, wife of Robert Hay the Egyptian traveller and archaeologist. Her story is rather exotic. In 1821, an uprising against the Turks was savagely repressed and Kalítza Psaráki and her brother Ioánnis (John) found themselves carried off from their home in Apodhoúlou and sold as slaves in Egypt. There, Kalítza was noticed by Robert Hay who, in 1828, bought and married her and later returned with her to Crete where he built the house with 'good English bolts'. Ioánnis stayed in Egypt, where he was eventually able to buy himself out of slavery. By the time Lear visited Apodhoúlou the couple had gone to Scotland and the house had passed into the possession of another brother of Mrs Hay's, Aléxandros Psarákis, and was steadily falling into disrepair. Aléxandros and his wife had seven children, one of whom (also called Aléxandros) acted as Lear's host. Tozer, visiting Apodhoúlou in 1874, found old Mr and Mrs Psarákis still alive but in 'reduced circumstances' after the uprising of 1866. The younger Aléxandros had by then emigrated to Marseilles where he held 'an excellent mercantile appointment' (*The Islands of the Aegean*, pp. 58–61). Another son stayed in Apodhoúlou as village priest and put up Arthur Evans overnight in 1894; the rabbits were still scurrying through the room (Joan Evans, *Time and Chance: The Story of Arthur Evans and his Forebears*, 1943, p. 315). Lear had known Robert Hay in Rome (he refers to him in 1858 as an 'old friend' — *Letters*, p. 124) but seems to have lost touch by 1864, since he needed to ask for his address. He must have intended to write to his old friend to let him know he had seen his Cretan in-laws but, as he discovered on his return to England, Hay had died the previous November. Pashley had also met Robert and Kalítza Hay (I, pp. 301–303).

83 Perhaps a variation of Tennyson, *In Memoriam*, CIV, 'The moon is hid, the night is still'.

84 *In Memoriam*, CIV.

85 Earl and Countess Somers were old friends of Lear's: 'He is a great favourite of mine, from my knowledge of many excellent points of his character, from our having many sympathies in common, and from our looking at many present-day matters with similar views. She is a most sweet creature. I think her expression of countenance is one of the most unmitigated goodness I ever contemplated. I call that a model of a woman. Bother: I wish they wern't [sic] Earls and Countesses — though I don't much care — for I've been so rummy independent all my life that nobody thinks I ever like rank for rank's sake I should think.' (*Letters*, p. 30.)

86 George's wife; George had originally come from Suli in Epirus but his family now lived in the village of Kastrádhes, near Corfu town. George had worked for Lear for four years — part of the time in Corfu itself — before telling him that he had a wife and children.

87 'O shame! he was a good fellow' (Lear's note, 28 July 1864).

88 Lear is imitating the Cretan accent with its 'tch' sound for 'k'; see note 69.
89 Printer of *Views in the Seven Ionian Islands*.
90 Mrs Clive's son, a Fellow of Balliol.
91 Brother of Reginald Cholmondeley of Condover hall, Shropshire; see *Letters*, p. 139.
92 A recent (1857) compilation of an Indian's memoirs: E. B. Eastwick, ed., *Autobiography of Lutfullah, a Mohamedan Gentleman; and his transactions with his fellow-creatures; interspersed with remarks on the habits, customs, and character of the people with whom he had to deal.*

GLOSSARY

aïdhónia (Greek): nightingales

alici (Italian): anchovies

atmópleon (Greek): steamer

baccalà (Italian): salt cod

baksheesh (Persian, current throughout the Middle East): gift, tip

basta (Italian): enough

bisacchi (Italian): saddlebags

borgo (Italian): hill-top town

bottarga (Italian): salted, dried fish roe

buca (Italian): cave

cacciatori (Italian): hunters

cadi (Turkish *kadı*): judge

caraba (Arabic *kharrubah*): carob

chibouque (French form of Turkish *çubuk*): pipe

cuccuma (Italian): coffee pot

Dogana (Italian): Customs

dolce parole (Italian): sweet words

dolmás (Greek): vine leaves stuffed with rice and often with meat

feriti (Italian): damaged

festa (Italian): feast day

fortómata (Greek): baggage

giro (Italian): tour

hegoúmenos (Greek): abbot

kalógheros (Greek): monk

kalos (Greek): good

kaphigi (probably Lear's mistaken transcription into Greek of the Turkish *καπιcι*): doorman or concierge

kastro (Greek): castle or citadel

kavass (Turkish *kavas*): armed servant or courier

khan (Turkish *han*): inn

kolokýthia (Greek): vegetable marrows

konak (Turkish): halting-place or staging-post

lordhos (Greek): lord, i.e. any wealthy European traveller

luogo (Italian): 'place', i.e. lavatory

metóhi (Greek): monastic dependency

mizzle (slang): decamp

moufflon: used by Lear to describe the Cretan *agrími* (wild goat)

mudir (Turkish): commander of a citadel

nargileh (Turkish *nargile*): hubble-bubble pipe, hookah

oka, plural *okádhes* (Greek and Turkish): measure of weight (just under 3lb) and of volume (about $2^1/_4$ pints)

osteria (Italian): inn

Othomanós (Greek): Ottoman, Turk

papás (Greek): priest

pastáhi (Greek): flour and milk dried in the sun to form a sort of *pasta*

piastre: French word applied to Turkish *kuruş,* a Turkish coin

piuttosto (Italian): rather

potius aper (mock Latin): rather + boar, i.e. 'rather a bore'

proestós (Greek): village president

rakí (Greek): colourless and highly potent spirit distilled from grape skins and stems left after pressing

ricotta (Italian): fresh white sheep's milk cheese

roba (Italian): baggage

salita (Italian): ascent

scomodi modi (Italian): inconvenient ways

scrivani (Italian): book-keepers

senza dubio (Italian): without doubt

shadoof (Arabic): pole with bucket and counterpoise used for raising water

spozalizio (Italian): engagement party

taphos (Greek): tomb

tavérna (Greek): inn

topos (Greek): place

trapézi (Greek): table

triglia (Italian): barbel

troppo (Italian): too much

SELECT BIBLIOGRAPHY

(The place of publication is London unless otherwise stated.)

WORKS BY EDWARD LEAR

Views in Rome and its Environs (1841).

Illustrated Excursions in Italy, 2 vols. (1846).

Journals of a Landscape Painter in Albania, etc. (1851); reprinted as *Edward Lear in Greece: Journals of a Landscape Painter in Greece and Albania* (1965).

Journals of a Landscape Painter in Southern Calabria, etc. (1852); reprinted as *Edward Lear in Southern Italy: Journals of a Landscape Painter in Southern Calabria and the Kingdom of Naples*, intro. Peter Quennell (1964).

Views in the Seven Ionian Islands, etc. (1863).

Journal of a Landscape Painter in Corsica (1870); reprinted as *Edward Lear in Corsica: The Journal of a Landscape Painter* (1966).

F[ranklin] L[ushington], 'A Leaf from the Journals of a Landscape Painter', *Macmillan's Magazine*, LXXV (April 1897), 410–430.

Lear in Sicily, intro. Granville Proby (1938).

Edward Lear's Indian Journal: Watercolours and Extracts from the Diary of E. Lear 1873–1875, ed. Ray Murphy (1953).

Lear's Corfu: An Anthology Drawn from the Painter's Letters, pref. Lawrence Durrell (Corfu, 1965).

The Complete Nonsense of Edward Lear, ed. Holbrook Jackson (1947).

Teapots and Quails, ed. Angus Davidson and Philip Hofer (1953).

Lear in the Original: Drawings and Limericks by Edward Lear for his Book of Nonsense, ed. Herman W. Liebert (New York and London, 1975).

Letters of Edward Lear Author of 'The Book of Nonsense' to Chichester Fortescue Lord Carlingford and Frances Countess Waldegrave, ed. Lady Strachey (1907).

Later Letters of Edward Lear to Chichester Fortescue (Lord Carlingford), Lady Waldegrave and others, ed. Lady Strachey (1911).

Edward Lear: Water-Colours of Greece . . . A Loan Exhibition . . . (1951).

Edward Lear 1812–1888: An Exhibition of Oil Paintings, Water-colours and Drawings, Books and Prints, Manuscripts, Photographs and Records, intro. Brian Reade (1958).

Edward Lear: Painter, Poet and Draughtsman: An Exhibition of Drawings, Watercolours, Oils, Nonsense and Travel Books (Worcester, Mass., 1968).

Edward Lear in Greece: A Loan Exhibition from the Gennadius Library, Athens, intro. Philip Hofer (Washington, D.C., 1971–2).

How Pleasant to Know Mr. Lear: Watercolors by Edward Lear From Rhode Island Collections, L. Candace Pezzera, Museum of Art, Rhode Island School of Design (Providence, R.I., 1982).

The Travels of Edward Lear, Fine Art Society (1983).

BOOKS AND ARTICLES ON EDWARD LEAR

Angus Davidson, *Edward Lear: Landscape Painter and Nonsense Poet (1812–1888)* (1938).

Philip Hofer, *Edward Lear as a Landscape Draughtsman* (Cambridge, Mass., 1967).

Vivien Noakes, *Edward Lear: The Life of a Wanderer* (1968; revised ed., 1979).

Joanna Richardson, 'Edward Lear: man of letters', *Ariel*, I (1970), 18–28.

John Lehmann, *Edward Lear and his World* (1977).

Thomas Byrom, *Nonsense and Wonder: The Poems and Cartoons of Edward Lear* (New York, 1977).

Anne Henry Ehrenpreis, 'Edward Lear Sings Tennyson Songs', *Harvard Library Bulletin*, XXVII (1979), 65–85.

Fani-Maria Tsigakou, 'Ὁ Edward Lear καὶ τὸ Ἑλληνικό τοπίο', *Ζύγος*, XL (1980), 52–54.

——*The Rediscovery of Greece: Travellers and Painters of the Romantic Era* (1981).

Ina Rae Hark, *Edward Lear* (Boston, 1982).

RELEVANT WORKS ABOUT CRETE

C. Rochfort Scott, *Rambles in Egypt and Candia, etc.*, 2 vols. (1837).

Robert Pashley, *Travels in Crete*, 2 vols. (1837; reprinted Amsterdam, 1970).

John Murray, *Handbook for Travellers in Greece: Describing the Ionian Islands, the Kingdom of Greece, the Islands of the Aegean Sea, with Albania, Thessaly, and Macedonia* (1854).

Bayard Taylor, *Travels in Greece and Russia: With an Excursion to Crete* (New York, 1859).

T. A. B. Spratt, *Travels and Researches in Crete*, 2 vols. (1865).

Georges Perrot, *L'Ile de Crète: souvenirs de voyage* (Paris, 1867).

Jules Ballot, *Histoire de l'insurrection crétoise* (Paris, 1868).

J. E. Hilary Skinner, *Roughing it in Crete in 1867* (1868).

V. Raulin, *Description physique de l'île de Crète*, 2 vols. (Paris, 1869).

William J. Stillman, *The Cretan Insurrection of 1866-7-8* (New York, 1874).

Charles Edwardes, *Letters from Crete: Letters Written During the Spring of 1886* (1887).

R. A. H. Bickford-Smith, *Cretan Sketches* (1898).

Raymond Matton, *La Crète au cours des siècles* (Athens 1957).

Pandelis Prevelakis, *The Tale of a Town*, trans. Kenneth Johnstone (Athens, 1976).

Elevtherios Prevelakis, *Ἡ Μεγάλη Κρητικὴ Ἐπανάσταση 1866–1869* (Athens, 1966).

Peter Warren, '16th, 17th and 18th Century British Travellers in Crete', *Κρητικὰ Χρονικὰ*, XXIV (1972), 65–92.

EDWARD LEAR'S ROUTE IN CRETE

Cape Spadha

Cape Akrotíri

Mon. Katholikó
Aghios Ioánnis
Mon. Aghia Triádha

Cape Vouxa

Ghoniá
Spiliá
HANIA Halépa
Cape Dhrepanon

Phalasarna
KISSAMOS
Dhrapaniá
Plataniá
Aghia Marína
Suda Bay

Aptera Arméni **RETHYMNON**

Palaiókastro
Ta Nopíghia
Kaloudhianá
Mourniés
Neohóri
Atsipópoulo
Adhele

Kaláthenes
Païdhohóri
Vamos
Dhramia
Pighí
Amnátos

Pemónia
Armyró
Perivólia
Mount

Topólia
Phré
Mon. Arkádhi

Lake Kourná
Episkopí
Mon. Asómatos

White Mountains
Amári Kastélli

Askýphou
Apodhoúlou
Va

Selino
Sphakiá
Sata

Tymbáki

Aghios Ioánn
Petró

Paximádhi

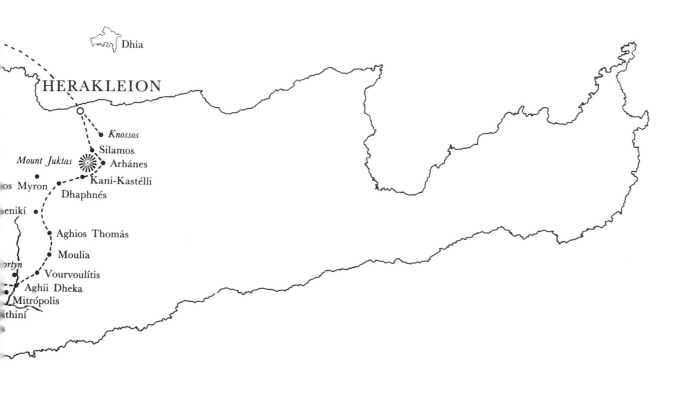

SEA OF CRETE

Dhia

HERAKLEION

Knossos

Silamos

Mount Juktas Arhánes

os Myron Kani-Kastélli

Dhaphnés

eniki

Aghios Thomás

Moulia

ortyn

Vourvoulítis

Aghii Dheka

Mitrópolis

thiní

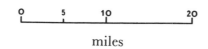

miles